S0-AQN-886

DADS, CATHOLIC STYLE

# Dads, Catholic Style

Bill Dodds

Servant Publications
Ann Arbor, Michigan

Copyright © 1990 by Bill Dodds
All rights reserved.

Published by Servant Publications
P.O. Box 8617
Ann Arbor, Michigan 48107

Scripture texts in this work are taken from the New American
Bible with Revised New Testament, copyright © 1986,
Confraternity of Christian Doctrine, Washington, D.C., and are
used with permission of said copyright owner. No part of the
New American Bible with Revised New Testament may be
reproduced in any form without permission in writing from the
copyright owner. All rights reserved.

Cover design by Michael Andaloro
Cover illustration by Jamie Adams

90 91 92 93 94  10 9 8 7 6 5 4 3 2 1

Printed in the United States of America

ISBN 0-89283-692-X

**Library of Congress Cataloging-in-Publication Data**

Dodds, William (Bill)
    Dads, Catholic style / Bill Dodds.
        p.      cm.
    ISBN 0-89283-692-X
    1. Fathers.   2. Father and child.   3. Catholic Church—
Doctrines.    I. Title.
HQ756.D57   1990
306.874′2—dc20                                    90-8894

# Dedication

*For my dad, John J. Dodds,*
*who taught me many things,*
*but especially how to laugh*

# Contents

# Being a Father Is Like Cleaning Out the Garage

BEING A FATHER IS A LOT LIKE cleaning out the garage. It seems like a really good idea when you start out—so optimistic and full of energy—but in no time at all you find yourself hip deep in:

— Christmas stuff;
— camping gear;
— a pair of studded snow tires to a car you sold three years ago;
— coffee cans overflowing with nails and bolts and little bits of God-only-knows what else;
— a power lawn mower (and weren't you supposed to drain the gas tank and change the oil before shoving it in here last fall?);
— several thousand paint cans with one teaspoon of paint in the bottom of each;
— a stack of old magazines that somebody in the house is saving for something;
— one hundred badminton rackets (but no net and the last shuttlecock is still in the gutter on the side of the house);
— enough bicycle parts to make a dozen unicyles but not enough decent parts to make even one good bike;
— a slow cooker, a fondue pot, and an electric knife sharpener;

— an assortment of empty boxes your wife is saving (DO NOT TOUCH THOSE BOXES!);

— a baby stroller without wheels;

— a half-completed, homemade go-cart with baby stroller wheels;

— a bunch of tools that should be hanging up on that really nice pegboard that you would have hung up on the wall if you had been able to find the tools you needed to hang it;

— your favorite flannel shirt that you haven't seen for two years (the one your wife—so innocently—says "must be in the back of the closet somewhere");

— a football that is as flat as that basketball that looks as pathetic as that baseball that has no cover; and

— a bunch of kids who are running around screaming and "helping Dad."

That, as you well know, is fatherhood.

That, dear Dad, is what this book is all about.

## WHAT KIND OF BOOK IS THIS ANYWAY?

*Dads, Catholic Style* isn't a "start at the beginning and read through to the end" kind of book. It's a "start anywhere, go anywhere" book. No bookmark required. I know you don't have a lot of time or a lot of quiet in your house. Maybe you can grab five minutes here or five minutes there. That's how this book should be read. That's why there are so many short chapters. (Forty-one! Count 'em! Forty-one! What a deal!)

In theory, the book's divided into three parts: One: Qualities of a Catholic Dad; Two: A Dad's Relationships; and Three: Special Times Together. Catholic fathers have some common traits (some they don't want and others they wish they had more of). Those qualities influence how a dad sees other people—especially his family—and how others see him.

Every dad's life also centers around a complex set of relationships that provide an abundance of challenges and joys. "Go ask your father!"

And for every father, there are times that are really tough and times that are really wonderful, truly priceless.

YES, BUT . . .

You may notice that one chapter or another doesn't seem to quite fit under any of those headings. I would agree. I've discovered that writing a book about fatherhood is also a lot like cleaning out the garage. You end up with a stack of stuff—good stuff—that doesn't really go into any of the piles (gardening, camping, tools, painting, St. Vinnie's, throwaways). Your wife won't let you start a "miscellaneous" box—and for God's sake don't use one of her boxes—because, really, it's all miscellaneous. So you toss the stuff in one pile or another and hope for the best.

You may also notice that time and again I write about "doing the little things." I think the little things—in being a father, in being a husband, in being a human—make up a big part of what's really important in life. Little things like saying please and thank you, helping my kids with their homework, or climbing a ladder to change a light bulb for Grandma.

There are a lot of Bible references in here, too. Don't let them frighten you. Being a Catholic myself, I had to look them up in a book called a concordance, which is like an index of words in the Bible. ("Samaritan, Samaritan, Samaritan. Now where the heck is the parable of the good Samaritan?")

And please keep in mind that I'm not claiming to be an expert on being a Catholic dad. I'm just a typical crew member on the good ship "Family." I just keep bailing.

*Part One*

# *Qualities of a Catholic Dad*

# ONE

# Peanut Butter and Paternal Instinct

A COUPLE OF YEARS AGO Andy was getting ready for his First Holy Communion and he had the assignment of drawing a picture of his family. I don't remember his impression of my wife Monica or our other two kids, Tom and Carrie, but I do remember me: I was the stick guy sprawled out on the sofa in front of the television set.

That was his dad.

He didn't mean any offense by it. He just drew what he saw.

That was a really busy time at the newspaper where I was working. I didn't see very much of Monica and the kids. When I did get home in the evening, I was so tired I'd just eat, watch television, and sleep.

I think every father has periods like that, when the pressures of work spill over into the home. Sometimes the pressures of home spill over into work. A dad lives in two worlds and they rarely split fifty-fifty right down the middle.

Sometimes one demands 75 percent of a guy's time and attention. And the other needs 80. Or more.

At least that's the way it seems.

So all a father needs to do is give 155 percent of himself. Simple.

A lot is said and written about maternal instinct. I don't recall seeing anything about "paternal instinct." I think there is such a thing, although I don't know how much of it is really a part of being a dad and how much is just something that our culture drives into us from a very early age.

The daddy goes out and makes money.

That's what it comes down to. He provides. In our society it isn't a warm cave and a chunk of meat. It isn't getting into a fight whenever an unfriendly tribe invades our territory.

In our society it's money for shelter and food and clothes. Those are today's basics.

But it's also money for soccer shoes and guitar lessons and VCR movies.

I know both parents in a lot of families have to work just to make ends meet. To try to make ends meet.

But most of us dads as little boys were taught that when we grew up, we had to go to work and take care of our wives and our children.

Women have done a good job of saying "I'm not June Cleaver." Men haven't done as well admitting they aren't Ward. They need to see that there's more to fatherhood than just providing the necessities—meaning material goods.

Sometimes going to work every day really stinks. Or as one older father put it: "I missed out on some wonderful times." There were Little League games and piano recitals and merit badge projects and grade-school open houses, but those were the exceptions.

Most of all, there were the "everyday" events: taking quiet walks, eating a bowl of popcorn in front of the TV, catching fireflies, sharing a laugh, a hug, or a good-night kiss.

A dad can joke that he's glad he didn't have to go to the Christmas pageant or the school play, but he knows he's missing something, something that's important to his son or daughter. So it's better to joke about it and then—somewhere in the middle of the kidding, kind of, sort of, in some way—admit feeling bad about missing it.

A fellow is lucky—blessed—if what he does for work is something he really likes to do. I think for most dads providing for the family comes before having the "perfect" job.

A father is living more than one vocation at the same time. Being a husband and dad—being a provider—should come first, ahead of a chosen career.

Sometimes it's hard to feel successful at that, especially when the money is gone or nearly gone even before the sun goes down on pay day. Not that it's wasted. Just spent. It takes a lot of money to keep a family going these days. Expenses always go up and raises don't always match them.

Sometimes providing means putting up with guff from bosses who make a lot of money but don't make a lot of sense. Sometimes it means trying to encourage staff members who think the world owes them a living. Often it's trying to please customers or clients who are not capable of being pleased.

Often being a father means you eat a peanut butter and jelly sandwich at your desk when other folks are going out to lunch.

It means you drive a car that would blend in well at a demolition derby.

It means you wear that old coat one more winter because your child needs a new one.

Sounds awful, doesn't it?

But somehow—most of the time—it isn't. When a dad stops to think about why it's peanut butter, a beat-up car, and an old coat, the answer is clear: it's for his kids.

Dads make all kinds of sacrifices for their children. They give up, they go without, they make do. That goes against society's grain these days. Comfort, luxury, and instant gratification are what we're all supposed to be striving for.

That's not fatherhood.

It never has been and never will be.

Many times, fatherhood is a daily grind.
But it's also a wordless prayer.
A noble calling.
A gift from God.

# TWO

# A Daddy Voice, A Daddy View

W HAM!
The newspaper hit the front aluminum screen door
with such force it made us all jump. We were in the living
room at my parents' house and were sitting around visiting
before dinner.

"I've asked him not to do that," Mom said.

"I'll talk to him," I told her as I hopped up and hustled out
onto the porch. The kid—maybe twelve or thirteen—was
already halfway to the next house.

"HEY!" I said. "YOU!"

He looked back at me.

"COME HERE!"

He took a couple steps my way.

Now, as every father has discovered, one of the advan-
tages of yelling at a child who doesn't know you at all is that
he or she will at least pretend to obey you. My own kids
would have just stood where they were and said "What?"
and "I didn't do it."

"Don't throw the paper so hard," I scolded him. "In the
summer, it could go right through the screen. In the winter,
it could break the glass. You can dent an aluminum door.
Did you know that? Do you have any idea how much it

would cost to replace an aluminum door? So from now on you walk around this bush and you toss the paper up onto the porch. You don't heave it over the bush and slam it into the door. You got it?"

He nodded.

"WHAT?"

He nodded faster.

"Thank you," I said.

I walked back into the living room and my brother and sisters burst out laughing.

"You sound just like Dad," one of my sisters said.

Dad looked at me and I looked at him and I thought, "Yeah, well . . ." and I bet he was thinking the same thing: sometimes you just have to talk to a kid and let him know what's what.

"You've never heard Bill use his 'Daddy voice'?" Monica asked and my siblings shook their heads.

"I have," Carrie said.

What was she doing in here with the grown-ups?

"I bet you've heard it a lot, haven't you, Carrie?" my mom asked.

"Mom!"

"Uh, huh."

I'll bet she has, too. So have Tom and Andy. I don't know any father who doesn't have a "daddy voice," who can't make "Hey!" sound like "I want you to stop that right now and get busy with what you're supposed to be doing, and I don't want to have to remind you again."

This is especially handy when time is at a premium. Say, for instance, Tom and Andy are doing the dishes and Tom says, "I saw a guy on TV who could juggle knives. He went like this."

Then there is "Come on." It's much easier to say those two words than to say "You're really not thinking this situation entirely through and the option you seem to be choosing may, in fact, be among the poorest choices."

They mean the same, of course.

It's my reply when Carrie tells Monica and me, "I'm not going to school today because my hair looks so dorky."

Another paternal favorite is the "exhale 'no' line." This is where a dad exhales loudly and quickly, and then says, no.

It shows that, even up to last breath I take, the answer will still be no.

"Can I walk over to the store with Kate? We each have three dollars."

"I get to wear these jeans to Mass because they're my good jeans. Huh?"

"I'll watch TV first and then I'll do my homework. OK?"

On the afternoon I spoke to the paperboy, another one of my sisters asked Carrie, "He doesn't whistle for you to come in when you're out playing, does he?"

"Go set the table," I said to my daughter.

"It's all done," Mom replied and smiled.

"Uh, huh," Carrie answered her aunt's question.

"I hated it when Dad did that," my sister said. "It made me feel like a dog."

"It works," I said, figuring there was no reason to argue with success. Dad agreed.

That led to a quick discussion of a mom who lived next door to us one time when we were kids. She would whistle four notes—a little tune she had made up—to get her kids home. It didn't take us long to learn how to imitate it. We had them running home all the time.

"You did that?" Carrie asked me.

"Me? No. Uncle Mike did."

"That was mean," she said and I said she was right, adding that I never did anything like that. No matter what Mike might tell her these days.

"Why not just call them by name?" my sister asked me.

"Whistling is faster," I said. "Easier."

I didn't mention that I hated to waste the six months of clarinet lessons I took in the sixth grade. That was when I learned a clarinetist and a shrill whistler hold their bottom lip in almost exactly the same position.

Fortunately for me, the conversation shifted that afternoon because it was time for dinner. God only knows what else—lies, half-truths and, worse than both, truths—my brother and sisters might have told my daughter.

We moved into the dining room and I sat down next to Dad. I felt close to him in a lot of ways. What he had said and what he had done when we were growing up were beginning to make more and more sense to me. I could see the love behind it all.

I don't just have a daddy voice, I have a daddy view.

That's how I look at the world now.

# THREE

# Fatherhood
# Is Like Tabasco Sauce

"JUST TASTE IT," I said to my three kids. "How can you tell if you like it or not if you don't taste it?"

In this case, "it" was Tabasco sauce.

We were at the dinner table, and I had put a drop of the spicy liquid on a bite of meat.

"You like hot salsa, don't you?" I argued.

They turned to their mom. Monica shook her head and said, "Not me."

I remember the first time I tried a slice of jalapeno pepper. This tiny green wheel sat on top of some cheese melted onto some tortilla chips. I popped it in my mouth and almost blew the top of my head off.

"I'll try it," my daughter Carrie said. Carrie who eats horseradish on her pot roast and blue cheese dressing on her salad. Carrie, the bold adventurer.

She took the bite and slurped down half a glass of milk.

Andy and Tom sided with their mother.

"It's good," Carrie said.

"What's it taste like?" Andy asked.

"Like . . . Like . . ."

"Like Tabasco sauce," I said. "There's nothing like it and the only way to know what it's like is to experience it."

That's true with a lot of things in life, I decided later.

9

Fatherhood, for instance.

Although I'd have to say that while being a dad is similar to a drop of Tabasco, it's even more like a slice of jalapeno. The things that come with it—responsibility, fear, anger, pride, love, exhaustion, near-bankruptcy—are enough to blow the top off any guy.

Fatherhood isn't for cowards. There's always something new that needs to be dealt with. One thing I've learned—that I'm learning—is that dads need to enjoy surprises and really like change.

It all begins when, just about the time you get used to living with a pregnant wife, the baby is born. Suddenly there's an infant in the house and how can such a tiny person take up so much time and energy and money?

I remember when Monica and I looked like cast members from "Night of the Living Zombies." Our darling infant didn't care if the sun was up or down and loved to play and eat and gurgle and squirm and cry from two to four just about every morning.

I almost got used to that and, what's this? There was a toddler running around and everything in the house that was valuable, breakable, or dangerous had to be locked away or put up on a shelf at least four feet off the floor.

A toddler soon becomes a preschooler who seems to spend most of his or her waking hours saying "Why?," "No," and "I don't want to."

Then it's on to kindergarten where a child prepares for "real" school by learning how to sit still, stay quiet, and follow directions. When I was younger and had no children, I thought it seemed silly for kids to spend nine months mastering those skills. When my own three hit that age, I thought nine months would never be enough.

Grade school covers a wide age range. For me, a nice part about having my children in grade school has been remembering friends and events from my own grade school days. It helps me understand their reluctance to finish a science project or a page of math when I recall my own mom dragging me to the dining room table and forcing me to complete a report on the Middle Ages.

Then come the junior high years, today often known as middle school. That's seventh and eighth grades, when members of the opposite sex suddenly become very, very interesting and a father becomes very, very stupid.

My kids used to think I knew everything. Now I'm fast moving toward "total airhead" in their estimation. At least I knew this one was coming. Monica and I have friends with kids who are teenagers or older. When we told these parents that two of our children were right on the edge of teendom they just laughed and said we would survive.

Probably.

I think we will.

"The teen years will go quickly, and then they'll be out on their own," a dad said to me. Then he smiled and added, "Although it won't seem that way when you're in the middle of it."

The years have gone quickly and the pace seems to be picking up. I miss the infants, toddlers, and preschoolers, kindergarteners, and primary-grade students I used to live with.

But I like the kids I share my home with now, even though they eat more, have more opinions, and are more inclined to point out my own shortcomings. I look forward to having high schoolers. College-age kids. Young adult children.

I like being a dad. There's nothing like it. No one can make me happier or more upset than my three kids who continue to help me turn to God in prayer. Quite often I find myself saying "Thanks" or "God help me! And them!"

I've found that being a father has never been boring. I suspect it never will be. A lot like a slice of jalepeno pepper or a drop of Tabasco sauce, my children have added zip to my life. They've given me much more than I will ever be able to give to them.

FOUR

# Everyone Is Afraid Sometimes

THE KIDS WERE VERY LITTLE WHEN they figured out "I had a bad dream" worked better than "open sesame." A preschooler would come padding into our bedroom in the middle of the night, say the magic words, climb over Monica or me and burrow between us.

Safe and warm.

I have to admit I was a bit of a soft touch because I frequently have nightmares myself, dreams that seem stupid or ridiculous if I remember them the next morning.

Monica likes to tell the story about when we were first married and I shot up in bed in the middle of the night and, still more asleep than awake, asked: "Are we alone?"

"I hope so," she answered.

Dads aren't supposed to be afraid. If there's a strange noise in the house after everyone has gone to bed, it's the father who has to go investigate. You cannot turn to your wife and say, "I support the Equal Rights Amendment. You go."

Well, you can, but it doesn't work. Trust me.

We live in a suburban tract house that was built about thirty years ago. The builders cut down most of the trees in the area, but left a huge evergreen in what was to become our front yard.

I'm pretty sure they didn't say, "Hey, someday Bill Dodds will be living here. Let's leave this monster out front to give him something to think about during bad windstorms."

The tree is healthy and there's no reason to think it's going to come crashing down in a high wind. Or to think that, even if it does fall, it's going to land on the house.

But still . . .

I never would have guessed that fatherhood is sprinkled with these vague fears.

What if Monica or one of the kids gets really sick or something worse happens to them?

What if I get sick and can't work?

What will my kids say—what have they said?—when another kid offers them crack?

What is society telling them when an eighteen-year-old can pick up a loaf of bread and an X-rated movie at the local grocery store?

How many teens die each year in alcohol-related accidents?

It does no good—in fact it harms my children—for me to be paralyzed with fear. But sometimes, late at night, as I'm drifting off to sleep, the wind blows hard.

And that big tree sways.

I need to remember my children have "trees" in their lives, too. There are things at school, in the neighborhood, and in our home that frighten them.

There are tough assignments and tough kids, tests and teachers, who seem to have it in for them on some days. There are friends on the block who suddenly side with another kid against them or who laugh at the stupid coat their father insisted they wear when it really isn't even that cold out. What if this spat between my mom and dad escalates? What if Mom or Dad moves out? What if they get a divorce?

I'm glad my children are afraid of some things. They should be. I need to instill that fear in them for their own safety. You don't get into a car with a stranger. You don't play football in the street. You don't go near a power line that's down. You don't ride your bike without your helmet.

I want them to fine tune that internal alarm system. I want it to ring loud and clear when they're in a situation that isn't safe. But I don't want them to cower under their beds. I don't want them to be so frightened that they never take a chance, never stand up and give it their best shot, knowing full well they may fall flat on their faces.

Never really live.

It's OK if you don't make the final cut on the wrestling team. It's OK if you draw a blank in the middle of reciting your memorized poem for the speech contest. It's OK if you stay right in the thick of the battle during a soccer game and accidentally kick the ball into your own goal, scoring a point for your opponent.

Every human being experiences fear. Even Christ—God and human at the same time—was afraid. On the night before he died, he took three of his closest friends to the Garden of Gethsemane. And, as St. Mark writes (Mk 14:32-36), a sudden fear came over him. He spoke to his dad. He prayed, "Abba, Father, all things are possible to you. Take this cup away from me!"

I don't want to do this! There has to be another way!

And then he immediately added, "But not what I will, but what you will." Even though he was afraid, Jesus did what God wanted.

My children have to do what God wants them to do. So do I. We can fuss and fight and fume, but in the end, we have to overcome the fears and do God's will. As if that's not hard enough, we have to take the time to figure out what God's will is.

There's another quote about fear that helps me when being a father is so scary. This one is in St. Luke's Gospel (Lk 12:22-32). Jesus is talking to his disciples.

". . . do not worry about your life and what you will eat, or about your body and what you will wear. For life is more than food and the body more than clothing. Notice the ravens: they do not sow or reap; they have neither storehouse nor barn, yet God feeds them. How much more important are you than birds! Can any of you by worrying add a moment to your lifespan? If even the smallest things are beyond your control, why are you anxious about the rest? Notice how the flowers grow. They do not toil or spin. But I tell you, not even Solomon in all his splendor was dressed like one of them. If God so clothes the grass in the field that grows today and is thrown into the oven tomorrow, will he not much more provide for you, O you of little faith?

"As for you, do not seek what you are to eat and what you are to drink, and do not worry anymore. All the nations of the world seek for these things, and your Father knows that you need them. Instead, seek his kingdom, and these other things will be given you besides.

"Do not be afraid any longer, little flock, for your father is pleased to give you the kingdom."

Take it easy, Jesus says to me. Remember what's important. Help your own little flock hear me, the Good Shepherd.

FIVE

# God's Love and
# Reading the Fine Print

"**C**ARRIE THINKS WE JUST WON $100,000," Monica said to me. "I have to run over to the store to get some stuff for dinner. Explain to her that we didn't."

That's another one of my "dad" jobs: throwing a wet blanket on some great deal one of my children has stumbled upon.

"Look!" Carrie said, showing me the evidence. She was holding a wad of information from a national sweepstakes envelope that had come in the mail. A sweepstakes that wanted me to buy magazine subscriptions.

"I scratched this junk off and got three that say $100,000," she argued. "It says 'You win any amount that appears three times.'"

"Uh, huh."

"So what's the catch?"

I love it when Tom, Carrie, or Andy asks that question. I want them to know there are some unscrupulous people in this world who will smile broadly and rob them blind. I learned that when I was nineteen. I was looking for a used car and I happened to answer a classified ad placed by a classmate from grade school who was selling one for five hundred dollars.

It was a jim-dandy 1963 Volkswagen squareback and I had to have it as soon as I saw it. Only later did my father's words come back to haunt me. "Never fall in love with a car."

But Dad let me buy it. It was my money, after all. And besides, the seller was a guy I knew from school who happened to work at a used car lot.

A week later, when I had to take it into the shop—a specialty shop that fixed VWs—it was still my money. Another three hundred dollars.

Another of Dad's sayings began to make sense: "A car will nickel and dime you to death." Only, I discovered, it wasn't nickels and dimes. It was twenty bucks. Fifty. One hundred.

I figure that car ended up costing me more than twelve hundred dollars. A lot of money in 1972 for a car that never worked right. I couldn't even afford to have all the repairs done. The guy at Joe's VW—we got to be on a first-name basis—showed me how to turn the ignition key on the right side of the steering column and then jam a screwdriver into the left to get the thing started.

Monica still talks about watching the sparks come flying out of that steering column.

Later I bought the family car from Mom and Dad. It was a '64 Chevy, an ugly workhorse of a car that needed little maintenance and probably is still running today.

I sold the vee-dub to a young woman who looked at it and fell in love. I explained to her all that was wrong with it which took quite a while. She didn't care.

It was cute. And, she assured me, her boyfriend could fix it all.

Since then I've thanked Dad for letting me buy that VW squareback. I was making the wrong decision, of course, but he let me make it. It was a twelve-hundred-dollar lesson I have never forgotten. That's dirt cheap compared to the price some people have to pay. Dad showed a lot of faith in me. He truly believed I'd figure out that I had been a real sucker.

So that was my background as Carrie stood in front of me and waved her certificate worth $100,000. "Did you read all the paperwork that came in that envelope?" I asked.

"Huh, uh." She shook her head "no."

"How about just the paragraph about the $100,000?"

"Yeah."

"Read it to me."

" 'Scratch off all the gold boxes, and if you have the lucky pre-selected number, you win any amount that appears three times.' "

I figured by then that she had mentally spent at least seventy-five grand. "*If* you have the lucky pre-selected number," I said.

"Huh?"

"See these numbers over here? It's like a raffle. Unless you get one of these, matching three numbers isn't worth the junk you scraped off them."

She smiled, pleased that she understood the catch.

"If it sounds too good to be true, it probably is," I told her, sounding a lot like my father talking about love and cars. "And," I added, "always read the fine print."

"There's always a catch, huh?" she asked. I hesitated. I want her and Tom and Andy to be wary, not cynical.

"A lot of times," I answered. "You have to be careful."

Later I thought of an exception.

A big exception.

The biggest.

It's God's love. God's love is perfect. It is unconditional. There's nothing I can do to earn it, and nothing I can do to stop it.

No matter what I do, God loves me.

That's how God loves my kids. That's how God loves every individual who's living, who ever lived, who ever will live.

The love I have for my children is imperfect. There are times when I am angry, times when I am tired, times when I have sinned—when I've made the wrong choice, when I've turned away from God. Those things influence my relationship with Tom, Carrie, and Andy.

I hope they know God loves them no matter what they do. Stopping his love can't be done. They have a better chance of standing in ankle-deep water at the ocean and telling the tide to stop coming in and out.

God is love, St. John the Evangelist says simply (1 Jn 4:16).

There is no catch, kids.

There is no fine print.

God loves you.

God loves me.

# SIX

# Tools of the Trade

I ALWAYS LIKE IT AT STATE OR COUNTY FAIRS when some guy or gal demonstrates an AMAZING! kitchen tool that chops, slices, dices, and juliennes—whatever that means. Usually the salesperson has a microphone strapped around his or her neck so the pitch can be heard from a quarter of a mile away.

"Your kids like french fries? Whoosh! There you go.

"Hate slicing onions? Zip, zip, zip! Now the only reason you'll be crying in the kitchen is if you burned the pot roast.

"Company coming over? One tomato, that's all you need. Just like that. Presto! You ever see slices so thin and so beautiful? I should look so good! You can feed a family for a week on that.

"So, what's something like this worth to you . . . ?"

What, indeed.

Not much. I like to putter around secondhand stores— being a dad, I spend a lot of time looking for bargains in secondhand stores—and I've come across a lot of AMA-ZING! kitchen utensils that don't work. That "razor sharp" blade might have cut a potato or two, but then it turned as dull as leftovers and couldn't be resharpened.

At the other end of the spectrum are the food processors. These are very expensive machines—often with French names like "Le Food Processor"—and they can do a variety of tasks. Chop. Slice. Dice. Julienne. And so on.

So can a knife. A kitchen knife. A plain old wooden-handled, steel-bladed kitchen knife.

Monica got a food processor for Christmas a few years ago. It—and it's thirty-seven parts—took up a lot of space in a kitchen cupboard for about eighteen months. Then it was demoted to a shelf in the garage, where it stayed until she gave it away.

It was too complicated and neither she nor I really cared if our cucumber slices were all exactly three-sixteenth's of an inch thick. We didn't need a lump of cheese grated in less than ten seconds. We seldom had to have walnuts chopped.

There's a weekly program on public television that features a guy who shows viewers how to make early American furniture without using any power tools. Yes, if he used a circular saw or a router he could save a lot of time and sweat, but the point isn't just the final product.

It's in the doing.

I'm not saying a carpenter should toss away all his tools that have to be plugged in or recharged. Those things involve his making a living. I use a personal computer to write. I don't sit down, light a candle, and pick up a quill pen.

But I don't want my kids to think they can't do something because they don't have the latest gadget or gizmo. I want them to come to understand that some things done by hand do not look "perfect" but are much more valuable. Both for the person who makes something like that and the person who receives it as a gift.

Teaching basic skills with basic tools—from parent to child or journeyman to apprentice—is something that has gone on for thousands of years.

It doesn't say so in the Gospels, but I like to imagine Joseph teaching Jesus about carpentry. Here's what this tool is for. Here's how it's used. This kind of wood is good for making this but not that.

It's not unreasonable to assume Christ followed in his

foster father's footsteps as a carpenter for part of the thirty years of his "private life."

What could be more natural?

Then he literally walked away from that and began a "public life." For three years he traveled throughout his homeland telling others about the kingdom of God. The distance between Nazareth, in the north, and Jerusalem, in the south, is only about sixty-five miles. But it was a long way from that carpenter's shop to the hill called Calvary.

On that day, now called Good Friday, the soldiers handed Jesus a cross and ordered him to carry it.

He did, of course, but first . . . First did he look at that piece of lumber and automatically note its dimensions?

Did he identify what kind of wood it was?

Did he think about what else it could be used for? How, with love and care and attention to detail, it could be transformed into a prized possession?

Did he think about his foster father as he unconsciously caressed it? Were there memories of the sweet smell of wood shavings, the thin crack of a board splitting along the grain, the gleam of a polished plane or ax?

Did his foster dad show him that there are no shortcuts when it comes to doing the job right?

He had a job to do with a wooden beam that day.

He did it right.

As I teach my kids about tools—saws and pliers, knives and computers, money and power—I'm teaching them about life, too. I need to keep in mind that I have the opportunity to share a lesson with them that can go way beyond the simple task we're trying to accomplish. I can help them come to realize it's in the doing.

# SEVEN

# Macho Man:
# The Strong, Silent Type

"WILL YOU OPEN THIS FOR ME?" Carrie asked as she handed me a new jar of pickles. I loosened the lid and gave the jar back to her. Later it occurred to me I had been the perfect father: strong and silent.

Before Rambo and Rocky there was Marshall Matt Dillon, John Wayne, and Gary Cooper showing what a real man was like. Everyone knows dads are supposed to be real men, not wimps. A good dad is the guy who says yep and nope and then gets busy looking after his woman and their young 'uns in a dusty old town way out West. Or a three-bedroom ranch house in the suburbs.

What a stupid stereotype.

One of the smartest men I ever met when it came to strength was a mentally retarded fellow named Bob. I was assistant director at a drop-in center for developmentally disabled adults and Bob would come by and shoot pool and listen to records and gab with anyone nearby.

The director had found someone willing to donate a kiln for pottery work. The only catch was we had to go get it. So we rounded up some of the bigger guys and drove over to the donor's house. We went down in the basement and came face to face with a kiln that weighed ... oh ... I don't know.

About a million pounds.

"Everybody get around it and we'll just try to lift it," the center director said.

OK.

"One, two, three, lift . . ."

It wasn't even an inch in the air when Bob said, "Too heavy," and let go. He walked back up the stairs and out of the house and got back into the truck.

He was right, of course.

We tried lifting the kiln again and eventually got it to the recreation center. We were lucky no one was seriously hurt.

Somehow it seemed better to risk injury than to admit I wasn't strong enough to be safely doing this. ("I wasn't strong enough" is a nicer way of saying "I was too weak.")

Real dads aren't supposed to be weak, physically or emotionally. They can lift anything and always keep their mouths shut because saying something out loud is a sign of weakness.

If I believe The Strong Silent Man is the perfect man then I'm not going to be a dad who says any of that "mushy" stuff. You know, stuff like:

— "I'm proud of you."
— "I missed you."
— "Thank you."
— "I'm sorry."
— "I love you."

Nope. Not me. Besides, I can tell myself, my kids know it anyway. I don't have to say it out loud.

That's true. I don't have to. Especially if I don't want to hear it said to me.

Unfortunately my kids learn a lot—bad and good—by what I do. If I never say "I love you" to them, it's not very likely they will say "I love you" to me.

Everybody loses.

But I know that can be hard to do. Harder if I haven't done it for a long, long time. And I need to remember that for a kid, even a couple of weeks is a long, long time.

I have to admit my three children are pretty suspicious if I spring it on them. When they're heading for bed, if I say, "Good night. I love you," they give me a look that asks, "What do you want?"

"I love you, and by the way, your room is a real pig sty."

"I love you, and you better get that grade up in math or you are dead meat."

"I love you, and if there's any messing around tonight you're going to bed half an hour earlier tomorrow night."

There has to be a catch, right?

I don't blame them. If one of them came running in from outside and said "I love you" and gave me a hug, I'd ask, "What did you break?" or "Who did you kill?"

Then, too, it's easy to argue that if I toss around those words all the time they will lose their meaning. They'll become like "How are you?" and "Have a nice day."

Maybe. But that's a pretty flimsy excuse.

Generally I know I'm in trouble when my wife Monica begins acting as a messenger between one of the kids and me. I volunteered to drive a carload of students from Andy's class on a field trip and Monica came to me and said, "Andy's really excited that you're going with him. He's looking forward to it."

Oh, yeah? That was the first I had heard about that.

"I'm glad I'm doing it, too," I told her. "I think it will be kind of fun." I presume she relayed the message. I don't remember what I said to him after the trip. Probably something like, "That was OK."

No doubt he answered, "Uh, huh."

Sounds like a John Wayne movie, doesn't it?

I think saying "I love you" is easy compared to saying "I'm sorry."

I hate to admit to my kids that I made a mistake.

They know I make a lot of them, but I hate to admit even one.

Yet I demand that they apologize when they mess up and hurt somebody else. Each one of them can make "Sorry" sound just like "Drop dead." They kind of spit the word out like it was sour milk or a bug or a fresh, green vegetable.

I bet they would be better at apologizing if they heard their father do it more often.

God the Father didn't stay quiet about his Son. In St. Matthew's account of the transfiguration (Mt 17:1-8), it says Jesus took Peter, James, and John up on a mountain and suddenly his face shown like the sun and his clothes were as white as light. Moses and Elijah appeared with him and Peter started babbling until God the Father shut him up. But first the Father said: "This is my beloved Son, with whom I am well pleased."

Try that in today's English:

"I love this kid. I'm proud of him."

That's the example I need to follow.

# EIGHT

# What Dad Has Time for Patience?

"STINKO!" I SAID as I punched one of the selection buttons on the car radio. And then another. And another. And another. "Nothing but stupid songs and sales pitches," I commented, but Carrie and Andy didn't say anything.

I was driving them to school that morning and since I've done that for years and years and years, they have learned to ignore me. On the other hand, I have quit quizzing them about who's singing a particular song. It was always some group from the '60s or '70s and they always answered the Beatles or the Monkees because they couldn't tell the difference between them.

The testing ended when they said the Monkees sang "The Sounds of Silence." Right.

But I like those radio buttons a lot. If there's a song that doesn't suit me or a commercial I don't want to listen to—SNAP!—it's on to another station.

The same with the remote control for the television set. I bet I'm not the only dad who spends Monday nights in the fall watching an NFL game and a situation comedy at the same time. And maybe some of the news, too.

I used to think I was a patient person. Maybe I was. But that was before I became a father. Now my patience seems to wear thin very quickly. Tom, Carrie, and Andy—whom I love dearly—make me angrier than anyone else in the world.

They are the only people in the world I yell at. (Except for maybe the occasional fellow driver and then only if I'm sure he can't hear me.) Not that yelling does much good except provide me with a little aerobic exercise.

"I'll bet you're the kind of dad who never shouts at his kids," a friend said to me one time. A friend who is not married and does not have children. Is there such a dad? I wondered. Has there ever been?

Sometimes my patience—or lack of it—seems like the brakes on the family station wagon. One summer we drove around the United States and it was late in the evening when we were heading through Zion National Park in Utah. It was a twisty, narrow, steep mountainous road that we were going down. Monica was at the wheel, and she was doing a great job.

We passed a car and could smell something hot like metal. "Their car must be overheating," I commented.

"Like we almost did going over that pass in Wyoming," Monica said, her eyes never leaving the road, her hands locked on the steering wheel.

"Lucky for us it was snowing that afternoon."

She laughed. There had been a lot of "adventures" on our 10,000-mile trip.

Another car passed us and again there was the hot smell. "Two of them!" I remarked.

"This is really steep," Monica said. "There's a place to pull off up ahead. I'm going to take a little breather." We were through the worst of it and it was a good thing: the smell was coming from our car. Our brakes. I'll bet they were so hot we could have used them to heat dinner.

We waited a while and then drove on. The brakes worked fine. It was just a bad combination: a steep downhill grade and a car overloaded with clothes, food, camping gear, and, roughly, ten million souvenirs.

That's the way it is being a father sometimes. I become overloaded and have to head up or down a big hill that puts a strain on the engine or the transmission or the brakes. My patience evaporates, and the kids drive me nuts.

Monica tries to help during those times. She says: "The kids are the same as always."

Translation: "It's you. Take a break."

If I go off by myself and watch a TV show or read for a while, the world looks a lot better. I no longer feel like ranting and raving at the kids. Just a little yelling and screaming. (I *am* their father, after all.)

I can see the same thing in the children. When one of them is overloaded and their brakes are starting to smoke. Then anything anybody does makes that individual mad, mad, MAD!

"He looked at me!"

"She started it!"

"He's being mean!"

"Does the whole world stink?" I ask that child.

"YES!"

"Everyone and everything?"

"YES!"

Then it's time for a break. Then I'm glad I took a break when I was ticked. People get angry. It's a fact of life. Part of my job as a parent is showing my kids what to do with that anger. How to handle it. How to live with it.

They also need to know that this kind of anger is pretty piddly stuff, but there's another kind, "righteous" anger. There are cases when I want my children to feel that. I want them to know that sometimes patience is not a virtue.

A lack of patience—an anger based on a demand for justice—was a spark in the Civil Rights movement in the United States.

In the dramatic changes in Eastern Europe.

In the realization in our country that women and children

are treated as things instead of persons when they are physically, even sexually, abused.

In the hearts of people who say, "Abortion is wrong. Fetuses are humans with dignity and self-worth and must be treated as such."

So how are my children supposed to know when to be patient and when to take action? How am I supposed to know?

That takes wisdom. That takes the Holy Spirit.

# NINE

# Sometimes It's Good to Be Proud

TOM WAS TWO DAYS OLD when he came to live with us. After being his foster parents for a while, we were able to adopt him. From the time Tom was very young, we've tried to instill in him a sense of pride.

We want him to be proud that he is racially mixed, Black and White.

Proud that he has two sets of parents, one biological and one adopted.

Proud that, although he has trouble learning, if he works hard, he can accomplish a great deal.

But all that came crashing down one day when Tom was in fourth grade. Other kids at school let him know, in no uncertain terms, that those were all things he should be ashamed of.

Tom came home crushed.

Angry.

Maybe feeling a little betrayed by Monica and me. This pride business, was it really like the tooth fairy? Was it a bunch of baloney for little kids only?

No. But we hadn't told him the complete truth: some people—often ignorant or wounded people—will try to put you down so that they seem higher. Make you out to be less so that they seem to be more, if only in their own eyes.

He came out of it stronger. And wiser. But Monica and I were worried when his whole eighth-grade class was going to put on a culture fair. Some three hundred fifty kids would set up displays in the school gym, each would be about his or her heritage or a family topic.

We let Tom decide what he would do. He displayed a world map showing the homelands of his parents' ancestors—adoptive parents and biological parents. Strings of yarn stretched from those places down to a photo of Tom. The table was filled with mementos and art work from the different countries.

Our son—looking more like a young man than a boy—stood next to his exhibit. He was decked out in an African chief's flowing robe and cloth cap, a souvenir Monica's brother had brought back from his time in the Peace Corps in Liberia. Tom stood tall, straight, and proud.

This is where I come from, he said wordlessly.

This is who I am.

For me, that was one of those comforting moments that don't come along very often as a parent. We must be doing something right, I told myself.

That's the positive side of pride. The kind I want Tom to continue to develop, the kind I want Carrie and Andy to have, too.

But then there's the negative side. Pride, after all, is one of the seven capital sins. (Along with covetousness, lust, anger, gluttony, envy, and sloth.) St. Thomas Aquinas said pride was number one.

The book of Proverbs puts it this way: "Pride goes before disaster, and a haughty spirit before a fall" (Prv 16:18).

Or as Carrie says: "Nobody likes a show-off."

So where does a dad draw the line? How does he point out to his kids that they need to have self-respect but not become braggarts? Not become experts at topping whatever anyone says or does?

Jesus said, "Love your neighbor as you love yourself."

"Love yourself."

Drawing that line isn't easy for me as a dad because it isn't easy for me as a person. Sometimes, I must admit, I take great pride in my humility.

What?

Humility comes from a Latin word, *humus,* which means ground or soil. Genesis describes God fashioning the first human from clay.

I don't want my kids to think they are dirt. I do want them to keep in mind what the priest traditionally says on the first day of Lent as he marks a cross with ashes on their foreheads. "Remember that you are dust and unto dust you shall return."

Maybe it would mean more to my children if our pastor said, "Don't be a hotshot."

Don't think that you can make it on your own.

Don't think you are better than everybody else.

Don't forget we're all in this together.

My kids need to remember that.

So does their father.

I also need to keep telling my children that I'm proud of them. I am. The desire to hear that, the delight that comes from hearing it, isn't something that's going to fade as they continue to get older.

I still like hearing it myself. I think I always will.

# TEN

# "Abba":
# God the Daddy

*A*BBA IS AN ARAMAIC word that's used to refer to God the
Father. But I've read that father isn't really a good
translation. Daddy would be closer.

*Abba* isn't a stern old man with a long white beard.

It's someone a child walks hand-in-hand with. Or, more
accurately, finger-in-hand. The way a dad walks with his
preschooler, when the child's entire hand neatly wraps
around a father's index finger.

I like the image of God the Father. It gives prestige to my
role. But it also gives added responsibility. In some ways,
how Tom, Carrie, and Andy look at God as a father depends
on how they look at me as a father.

Let's see. That must mean God yells when somebody
doesn't take out the garbage, that God says no TV until the
homework is done, that God doesn't have to eat vegetables
when he doesn't want to.

The Bible is loaded with the image of God as father. When
Christ's disciples asked him how to pray, he began his
prayer with "Our Father."

That's a really radical idea, but most of us are so familiar
with it that it's lost a lot of its punch. Imagine a God, the one
who made everything, telling some of his creatures, "You
are my children."

His children!

He is our father. He is the one who provides, who protects, who encourages, who scolds. He's the one who understands, who forgives, who points out the bright side. He's the one who loves us. Individually.

I am the father of Tom, Carrie, and Andy and that gives them a special bond. (At times, it might seem to them, a common enemy.) Clearly, they are brothers and sister.

This "Abba" is the father—the daddy, the papa—of all those in Christ. Clearly, or often not-so-clearly, it makes us brothers and sisters. Christ gives us a bond, a relationship, an interdependence that can't be ignored. Not if a person wants to be happy. Wants to be at peace.

I want my kids to remember that people on the other side of the world, people they will never meet, are their brothers and their sisters. My kids can't ignore what's happening to those folks anymore than they could ignore what's happening in their own home.

They can choose to ignore that, both inside our home and outside it, but they shouldn't. If Tom isn't feeling well, then Andy and Carrie need to adjust to that. If Carrie is worried because of something that's happening at school, Tom and Andy have to keep that in mind. If Andy is down because his soccer team got clobbered, Tom and Carrie have to take that into consideration.

Part of what a dad does is instill in his kids a sense of responsibility for one another. We are a family. We stick together. Although, being a typical family, sometimes we feel more like giving each other a swat on the head than a pat on the back.

One time, for a newspaper article, I was covering a theologian's speech. He said a lot of stuff that went right by me, but one thing stuck. He said people tend to think: you are human to the degree that you are like me. If there are a lot of differences—race, religion, class, nationality, location—then you are unlike me and so are less than human.

Those were hard words, but I think he was right. That's something I have to fight within myself. I have to show my kids that way of thinking and acting is contrary to a people that has a common "abba."

It's a sad fact, but some kids are growing up without a father or, worse, they're growing up with a father who is abusive. It's not surprising that these kids—now and as they grow older—may want little to do with a God who is a father. It's not surprising that if that's one of the dominant images the church uses to describe God, they may want little to do with the church.

I don't think that means we should abandon that powerful and beautiful image. I think it means I, as a dad, have a responsibility to demonstrate what a father can be. In every community, in every neighborhood, in every parish and school, there are single moms raising kids. One way I can help is by being a good dad to my own kids. Other kids—classmates, neighbor kids, friends—are going to see that and it's going to give them another image of father.

It doesn't mean I must become their father.

It doesn't mean their future depends on me.

In many ways, it's doing the little things that can have a big effect. It can help them see this God, this "abba," who is their daddy just like he's my kids'.

Just like he's mine.

# ELEVEN

# Learning to Be Compassionate and Forgiving

W HEN THE KIDS TALK ABOUT their career plans, none mentions "save the world." I don't know if they're smarter than Monica and I were or just not as idealistic.

We were going to save the world.

Well, really, since there were two of us, each of us was going to save half. We'd be done twice as fast. Of course, that was when I was younger and knew all the answers. Now enough years have passed so that I realize I know very little.

Answers? No way. On a good day I might have a glimmer at some of the questions.

Life isn't a matter of enjoying the answers. It's learning to live with the questions.

As for saving the world, that position's been filled. God sent his Son to handle that one. I may do well at some things, but I don't want to try to match resumes with Jesus.

It used to be that resumes were pretty much a straight chronology: first I worked here, then I worked there, and then I worked somewhere else. Now some experts advise job-seekers to divide their resume according to specific skills. Supervising others. Managing a budget. Meeting deadlines. Keeping customers happy. And so on.

I think Jesus' resume would have included a section for "showing compassion." "Jesus was moved to pity" it says in the Gospels. Jesus felt sorry for people in need. Jesus' heart ached a little bit and he offered his help.

He healed the sick.

He fed the crowds.

He touched the leper and cured him.

He was touched by the sight of a widow whose only son had died. He stopped the funeral procession and raised the young man from the dead.

Look at what this Jesus can do, I need to tell my children. Even today, he can heal you. Feed you. Touch and cure you. Bring back to life things—relationships, ideals, emotions—you thought were dead.

Great! Let's end the discussion on compassion right there. How comforting. But, as always, there's more. This is what Christ did and this is what his followers must do.

What my children must do.

What I must do.

In the parable of the unforgiving servant (Mt 18:21-35), Jesus says the kingdom of God is like a king who decided to settle up with his staff. One poor fellow owed thousands upon thousands of bucks. "You seem to have caught me at a bad time," he told the king. "You're going to be sold," the king answered. "You and your wife and your kids and your property."

"Please!" begged the servant, "cut me some slack. I'll pay it all back. I just need a little time."

The king was "moved with compassion." He let the guy go and wiped out the debt.

What a great story, huh, kids?

Unfortunately, there's more.

The servant—a middle manager, evidently—went out and grabbed a fellow servant by the throat and said, "Pay up!" The second servant owed him a few bucks. He dropped to his knees and begged, "Cut me some slack. I'll pay it all back. I just need a little time."

But the first servant wasn't buying it. He had Number Two immediately tossed in jail. Someone went back to the king and spilled the beans. The king called the first servant in and said, "What the heck is going on here? I forgive a debt of thousands upon thousands and you can't eat a few bucks?" Then the king handed the servant over to the "torturers" to work him over until he paid off all he owed. Which, considering the amount, would take about forever.

"My father is like the king," Jesus said. "You're like the first servant. Whatcha gonna do?"

Will my kids follow the king's example? Will they be moved with compassion and offer forgiveness?

My children will not save the world, but they can help other people. A lot of people need help. I want my children to be sensitive to those needs. Matthew writes about Jesus' compassion, too (Mt 9:35-38). He says Jesus was going around doing good things and "At the sight of the crowds, his heart was moved with pity for them because they were troubled and abandoned, . . ."

That was when he told his followers, "The harvest is abundant but the laborers are few; so ask the master of the harvest to send out laborers for his harvest."

*Troubled* and *abandoned* could be used to describe a lot of people today. There's still a lot of work to do.

I want my children to be among those laborers. I want them to be moved with pity, to have compassion for their fellow humans and then act on those feelings. Part of my duty as their father is leading them into that field. It is true that sometimes it feels less like I am leading them and more like they are pushing me. But in either case, part of the joy I feel as their father comes from serving side-by-side with them. A large part of that joy.

# TWELVE

# Everybody Has Rules to Follow

WHEN I TELL MY KIDS TO DO SOMETHING they, like all kids, have a tendency to ask "Why?" And I, like all dads, always have an answer. A lot of times that answer is: "Because I said so." I didn't say I always have a good answer, just an answer.

I bet there isn't a father on the face of this planet who hasn't answered a question with "Because I said so." I agree that you have to explain things to your kids, but sometimes it's very obvious they are trying to slip into a stall pattern. They begin to sound like a tricky lawyer filing motion after motion so that his client never has to actually come to trial.

"Why do I have to go to bed?"

Oh, I don't know. Maybe it has something to do with the fact that it's your bedtime.

"Why do I have to clean my room?"

To settle an argument your mother and I are having. We can't remember if your floor is carpeting or hardwood.

"Why do I have to do my homework?"

"Why do we have to come in now?"

"Why can't we play videos?"

Why?

Why?

Why?

Sometimes my answer makes sense to them. I can tell. Not because they say, "Oh, that makes sense! Yes, I'll get on that little task right now!" No, not that. It's because they quit arguing. Quit presenting their case.

"Why do I have to go to bed now?"

"Because your bedtime was forty-five minutes ago."

Monica and I are the first authority figures our kids run up against. We set the rules for them. Sometimes they agree with those rules and sometimes they don't.

Sometimes it matters to us if they agree and sometimes it doesn't.

Sometimes they have a say in determining those rules and sometimes they don't.

Part of my job as a dad is teaching my kids that life is full of rules. Absolutely jam packed. At home, at work, on the road, in the neighborhood, in the store . . . everywhere.

"Eight items or less. Cash only. This checkout stand."

"One way."

"Envelope must be postmarked no later than April 15."

And they aren't always written down. Our garbage cans have to be out by the street first thing Wednesday morning if we want the garbage collector to haul our stuff away.

Some rules are laws, some are customs, and some are just common sense. (I cannot walk into a bank with a pistol and say, "I'd like to make a withdrawal." I shake hands with someone when I first meet him or her. I brush my teeth twice a day.)

But some people—adults—have a horrible time with rules, with authority. It doesn't matter what's said or who says it, they're against it. And they spend a lot of time and energy trying to get around it.

I don't mind that my children question the rules. I just hope they learn that some rules they can change and some they can't. ("I don't believe in gravity!")

I hope they learn that in a democracy they have a say in determining those rules. There is a way to challenge those rules and to change them. Authority, ultimately, rests in the people.

I know it's hard for them to appreciate what that means. If you grow up in a democracy, you tend to think that's the way it is everywhere.

I began to see the beauty in our system when I became an editor of a weekly Catholic newspaper. It dawned on me that in some countries I would be imprisoned or shot for what I did. That became how I would "test" a country, whether its government leaned to the left or right. Could I head a staff publishing a Catholic newspaper there? How do they treat the press? How do they handle religion? What would be my life expectancy there?

The church is an authority, but that doesn't mean it's nothing more than a set of rules. It's not a democracy. I can't round up a majority of people and vote out the fact that during the celebration of the Mass bread and wine are transformed into the body and blood of Christ.

The church helps me develop what's called an "informed conscience." That means that, because God has given me free will, I'm the one who must decide what I do. But I don't make those decisions with my head up in the clouds or buried in the sand. I don't ignore what the church teaches because it's there to help me answer the very hard questions life forces me to ask.

I hope my kids come to realize that no matter who you are or what you do, you have to answer to someone.

You have to answer to yourself.

And you have to answer to your God.

# THIRTEEN

# Life Was Made for Laughing

M Y EIGHTY-SIX-YEAR-OLD grandmother adjusted the bow in her hair, one of those ready-made jobs you slap on a gift after you've wrapped it. "Let's see some apple cheeks," I said and she blew out her cheeks as round as she could make them, which was very, very round. It did look like she had two apples tucked away in there. She wasn't senile; she always acted that way.

That was in the spring of 1983 when I was able to visit her in Milwaukee. It was the last time I saw her. It's a very happy memory. Grandma died the following March. She had been a widow since she was fifty-six. After grace before meals, Grandma always added an extra prayer for the souls of the faithful departed.

She spent a lot of time each day praying. She had a wad of prayer cards and novenas and such that she would say daily. Her prayer books were tattered from constant use. Grandma told me one time that a priest had said one thing widows can do is pray for everyone else. She took his advice seriously. It always seemed to me that her death—her moving from this life to the next one—had to be about one of the smoothest transitions anyone ever experienced.

That was my grandmother. The one with the gift-package

bow stuck to the top of her head. She liked to pray and she liked to laugh. That's what I want for my kids, too. I hope that's the kind of home we have here. Religion isn't a wrathful God with long-faced followers. I believe in a God who created humor and I believe there's good reason to laugh at a lot of what he created and at the messes I tend to create for myself.

Often in life, the choice is laugh or cry. Most of the time it's better to laugh. But not always. Sometimes the tears come. Pain and grief and worry, sadness of all kinds, are a part of life, but they are not the whole of life. With God's blessing they fade and, as they do, the laughter returns.

I write a lot of humor pieces, and people ask me if it's hard to do. Not at all. I find it easiest. That's how I look at life, and I hope it's how my kids will look at it. I hope that's something I can pass on to them. I know it's something I received from my father.

Dad cultivated a sense of humor in each of us, my sisters and my brother and me. We were encouraged from a very early age to be funny. Except for the occasional barb or two thrown at a sibling, the humor was never mean. It was never dirty, never poking fun at ethnic groups, never jokes about old people, or jokes about people with disabling conditions.

I was in high school when I figured out humor could be a good defense to diffuse people's anger. I remember the time I had borrowed another guy's football cleats for an intramural game, without asking permission. I didn't think he was playing that afternoon, but I was wrong.

He came storming out onto the field, followed by a few others who wanted to see what he was going to do to the poor, dumb thief who had walked off with his equipment. He was a big guy. I wasn't a big guy, I just had big feet. I also had big trouble.

"I promised I was going to punch out whoever took my shoes," he growled, looking me right in the eye.

"Don," I answered slowly, trying to sound sincere, trying

to sound like my only concern in the world was making life easier on him, "I'm not going to hold you to that promise."

The onlookers laughed, he laughed, and I was spared.

Later in life, when I became a boss, humor helped me work with people. It was an attitude that created an atmosphere that said, "We can take what we do seriously without taking ourselves seriously."

I hope my kids can always laugh at themselves. I hope I give Tom, Carrie, and Andy enough self-confidence and enough love so that they can admit they make mistakes, admit they do some incredibly stupid things.

They do, of course. They're following right in their father's footsteps.

As I continue to try to follow in my dad's.

Laughing as we go. Happy to be here.

*Part Two*

# *A Dad's Relationships*

# FOURTEEN

# Fathers and Sons

A FEW YEARS AGO I WAS going to take Tom and Andy to an indoor auto race, but a snowstorm forced us to cancel our plans. The three of us had really been looking forward to seeing a pickup truck with monster wheels smash its way across the top of a string of cars.

Instead, a couple of weeks later, we went to an auto show. That's where we saw it.

We had wandered around for a while and scooped up a lot of free key chains and bumper stickers when we spotted it in the middle of the exhibition hall: the "General Lee." It was the car used by Bo and Luke Duke on the old television show, "The Dukes of Hazzard," that bright orange Plymouth with the Confederate flag painted on its roof.

My two sons stopped dead in their tracks. They loved that show. They loved that car. We walked over to it slowly and they reached out and touched it gently.

"The General Lee," Tom whispered reverently.

"Yeah," Andy answered the same way.

We saw lots of other things that day, but kept circling back to see that orange Plymouth just one more time. I'm glad I didn't tell them probably a half dozen or more cars just like it were used for the TV program. I'm glad I didn't say it was just a hunk of metal, a machine. It wasn't.

It was the "General."

They still talk about it. It's a good memory for all three of us. Something the guys did. I think it's important that sometimes there's a boys' night out. We have nothing against Monica and Carrie. We like them. But sometimes . . .

I remember going to the Golden Gloves boxing tournament with my father and my brother when I was a kid. Twice. Well, only one time, really.

Dad boxed in high school and has always liked the sport. As children, the five of us learned not to sit too close to him when he was watching a fight on TV. He couldn't sit still. He was always ducking and jabbing.

I remember the first Golden Gloves. It was a big deal because Mom and the girls weren't with us and we were downtown after dark on a cold winter night. "That's where we're headed," Dad told us two boys and pointed at a light on a building. "That sign up there."

"What sign?" I asked him.

I was in the sixth grade. It was when Dad discovered I needed glasses.

The second time—when we almost made it to the tournament—was a couple of years later. We were pretty new to Seattle then. Major events were held down at the Seattle Center, in either the Coliseum or the Arena. They're at opposite ends of the grounds.

Dad walked up to the ticket office and was pleased to discover this was going to cost him less than he had planned. He bought one adult and two kids' tickets and we walked in . . . to the Big Seattle Boat Show!

Wall-to-wall vessels and nautical gadgets.

Mike and I had a great time. When you're that age, the destination doesn't matter so much. It's the journey that's a hoot. A boat show is just as good as a boxing tournament.

Maybe better. There's a lot of free stuff at a boat show.

"As soon as I walked in, I knew I was dead," Dad said years later as he told the story. Come to think of it, I'm not sure he ever told the story on his own. Mike and I are usually the ones who bring it up. And laugh. Dad meant that he was sure he couldn't get a refund on the tickets. Since he's good about getting his money back when it's at all possible to get his money back, we figured he was right.

I think all fathers want to have good times with their sons—create happy memories—but money does put a limit on choices.

Not too long ago Tom and Andy and I tried to get to another car show. It featured racing and monster trucks and a demolition derby and all sorts of neat stuff. Then I priced the tickets. It would have cost us forty bucks.

No way. I hadn't really thought about what our limit would be, budget wise, but I was certain that was over it. Way over it.

"Sorry," I told them, "but we can't afford it."

They said they understood. They said it was OK.

Then, about a week later, Monica was out one evening and Carrie wanted to watch some music show on TV at the same time that a sports-bloopers/big-plays special was on. I had seen some commercials about it and knew Tom and Andy would enjoy it, and that I'd enjoy watching it with them. We guys didn't really banish Carrie to the other room and the little television set. We just suggested she move in there.

Then I popped a blank VCR tape into the machine, punched the record button, and we ate popcorn and watched the show. (Carrie wandered out for some food but didn't stay for the program.)

There were seven-foot basketball players crashing into metal folding chairs as they dove to keep the ball in bounds. Center fielders climbing walls to make spectacular home-run-stealing grabs. Twenty-two NFL players—with a combined salary of God-only-knows how much—who couldn't find the handle on a fumbled football. It was great.

Maybe a month later—on a wet and cold afternoon—Tom and Andy and a friend sat in the living room and laughed and shouted as they watched the videotape. I sat down for a minute or two and watched it, too. But mostly I just watched my sons.

# FIFTEEN

# Fathers and Daughters

"YOU'RE GOING TO WEAR THAT?" my daughter Carrie has said to me on more than one occasion. A lot more. And the tone in her voice, the way she emphasizes "that" and stresses the question mark, lets me know that I better not really be considering wearing whatever it is.

At least not in public.

Not in public with her. Not in public where any of her friends might see me and know who I am in relation to her. Not even if I promise that, should I run into one of her friends or classmates, I would say, "Hi! I'm not Carrie's dad."

Not even then.

Carrie's "that" could be a comfortable old sweater, a warm knit cap, a pair of wild summer shorts.

Not all at the same time. Not usually.

The point is, we have a different sense of fashion, my daughter and I. For instance, I believe coats should be zipped up when it's snowing, raining, or below freezing.

She does not.

I believe you could wear a hat on the playground at school. That you do not have to stuff it into your backpack as you step out of your father's car first thing in the morning.

She does not.

I believe a person could survive without combing his or her hair every ten to twelve minutes.

She does not.

One of the delights of having a daughter is living with someone who still has faith that you are not beyond hope. Not beyond being helped. That with just a little work and a little, well, brains, you could look (and act and talk and think) all right.

That's part of a father-daughter relationship. Kind of a fun one.

There's also the part where my daughter tries so hard to please me. I know she does. I know she loves me very much and she wants to be sure that I love her and that I am proud of her.

She wants to make me proud of her.

I am. I hope she always knows that. I hope I always let her know.

There's the part of our relationship that sometimes she believes me more than she does her mother. Moms always say you're good looking and a nice kid and all that stuff. It can mean more to her when I say, "You're pretty."

"You look nice in that outfit."

"Your hair looks good that way." (Without adding, "SO JUST LEAVE IT ALONE!")

In some ways it's harder to be the father of a girl than it is to be the father of a boy. I used to be a boy. I can remember playing tackle football in the mud and digging for worms and hating girls. Sort of hating them but being very interested in them, too. An interest that just kept growing and growing as my fascination with mud football and worm hunts faded.

Through it all, girls were a mystery. How they thought and what they liked to do and how they acted and just everything about them.

They still are a mystery, my wife and my daughter. They go off and do things together. Girl things. They go shopping at the mall and they get their hair done. And they never invite the guys or me. They never say, "We're going to go look for shoes. Do you want to come along?"

I'm not trying to promote a war between the sexes here or say that men are better than women. Or women are better than men. I am merely commenting that my wife and daughter have never asked me to go look for shoes with them.

If they did, I would say no.

I could understand going to "buy" shoes. If you need shoes, you buy shoes. I do not understand going to "look for" shoes. I already know where shoes are. They are in the shoe departments or shoe stores.

They do not invite me because I would say, "Oh, look, we found the shoes. Now, you going to buy a pair or not?"

So Monica and Carrie go on those little outings alone, but my daughter and I do other things together. Neutral things. Bookstores, for example. We can go to bookstores together. We can go for walks. We can watch the VCR tape of Lucille Ball and Desi Arnez in "The Long, Long Trailer." We can talk about what a pigpen the boys' room is.

I want my daughter to grow to be a woman of faith. Like her mother. Like her grandmothers. I want her to know that the history of the church is filled with stories of strong women of faith. That in so many times, in so many lands, in so many homes, it has been a Catholic woman who has nurtured the gift of faith.

Women showed that faith when Jesus was on earth. Some would step up and ask him for his help. One didn't even ask (Lk 8:43-48). She thought, "If I just touch the hem of his garment, I can be cured."

Amazing. And, of course, she was right.

There were women who heard him speak and became his disciples, following him from town to town. There were women who watched and cried as he carried his cross. Women who were at his feet as he died that horrible death

(Mt 27:55-56). Women who didn't run and hide the way all but one of the apostles did.

Women who saw where Christ was buried and said they would come back to prepare the body properly after the Sabbath (Lk 23:55-56). Women who did return, even though they weren't sure how they were going to get the big rock out of the way to get into the tomb (Mk 16:1-3). No matter. They would handle it somehow.

Instead the rock had already been moved. The tomb was empty. An angel was there. They ran back to tell the apostles.

Jesus first appeared to a woman after he had risen from the dead (Jn 20:11-18). Mary Magdalene didn't recognize him at first. She thought he was the gardener and, please, if he knew what had happened to the body, would he tell her?

Then Christ said, "Mary."

She recognized him and answered, "Teacher."

That's what I want for my daughter. I want her to go looking for Jesus and find him standing there. I want her to hear him call her by name.

I want her to answer.

# SIXTEEN

# My Children's Mother

THERE ARE TIMES WHEN MY CHILDREN come to me because they are fighting about something and they want my advice. They want me to listen to all sides of the argument and then render a decision which is fair and acceptable.

That means each wants me to say he or she is absolutely, 100 percent right and the opposition is totally bonkers.

Like all dads, I have learned how to handle this. Before they get three words out, I say: "Go ask your mother."

I love my wife dearly, but maybe never more than when I can move the Family Court into her jurisdiction.

She can do the same. When she's tired or busy or worried or just doesn't want to play referee/judge/peacekeeping officer. Then she can say, "Go ask your father."

We are a team, she and I. Maybe that gives the impression that sometimes family life is "us" (the parents), against "them" (the kids).

It should give that impression. Sometimes that's exactly what it is. They have us outnumbered. They are younger and, day by day, growing stronger. We need to rely on our wisdom and our cunning. They have more stamina than we do, but we can make them eat broccoli.

The kids know that sometimes it is us against them. That's OK. Good, in fact. Because then they can see that their mother and I are partners.

Teammates.

Friends.

They can see that marriage isn't just loving someone else, it's liking that person. Wanting to spend time with that person. Having fun with that person.

I hope Tom, Carrie, and Andy see that and realize love is more than passion, more than sparks. That's part of it, of course, but love is also a steady flame. A constant source of light and heat.

I've never said to them, "This is how you should treat your spouse when you grow up," but every day I try to show them.

What am I teaching them? A mother is just a cook? A chauffeur? A bookkeeper? A laundress? A maid? A nanny? A wage-earner? A gardener? A tutor?

I hope not. She may cook, drive the kids places, balance the checkbook, wash the clothes, keep the house in order, take care of the children, work outside the home, keep the yard in shape, and supervise homework.

And more. A lot more.

But she isn't doing those things for money. (The kids and I couldn't afford to pay Monica for all she does.) She's doing them because she loves us. That's part of what a mother and wife is.

And the kids should see I'm doing many things right alongside her. That's part of what a father and husband is.

We're a team.

My children can also see that I'm not just a dad, but I'm also still a son. How I want them to treat their mother—the respect and love I want them to show—is how I should be treating my own mom.

That can mean doing such little things. So much of life— what's really important—is the little things. It's getting up on a stepstool and putting a new lightbulb in the hallway fixture when we're over visiting. It's shopping around to get just the right present for Mom's birthday. (Or, better yet, making something and having the kids make something, too.) It's stopping by for no special reason except to say hello.

I want my children to honor their mother. Just like the commandment says. The first three commandments have to do with a person's relationship to God. ("I am the Lord, thy God, thou shalt not have strange gods before thee. Thou shalt not take the name of the Lord, thy God, in vain. Remember to keep holy the Lord's day.")

But number four, the first one talking about fellow humans, has to do with parents: "Honor thy father and thy mother."

I don't try quoting the father part to my kids. I'm sure they would quickly counter with Colossians 3:21: "Fathers, don't nag your children." No kidding. That's what it says. It may be the only Bible quote my children know.

It's from one of the readings for the feast of the Holy Family, the Sunday between Christmas and New Year's. I remember one year my brother was visiting on that day and so we had a home Mass. My sister Mary was a lector. When she hit that passage she slowed way, way down and looked right at me.

Hmmm, . . .

That's part of family life. The good-natured teasing. The laughing that's based on a grain—or more than a grain—of truth. It's being together and sharing the laughter, admitting imperfection, and sharing the love.

I hope my kids always have that kind of relationship with their mom. I hope they always appreciate what a wonderful person she is.

# SEVENTEEN

# All Kids Aren't Created Equal

"**H**ERE'S A GOOD GENERAL RULE if you're ever doing the grocery shopping and the kids start begging for a certain kind of breakfast cereal," Monica said to me one day after she had returned from a trip to the supermarket.

"OK," I said.

"Never buy one named after a cartoon character or comic book hero. It may say 'low sugar' on the front, but the list of ingredients on the side is going to have fructose, corn syrup, honey, and every other kind of 'non-sugar' sugar there is."

"Right," I said. "Check the ingredients."

It would be a lot easier for me to be a father if my children had a list like that. If they came with their ingredients printed on them, telling me what they have the most of and the least of.

Is "mechanical ability" listed before "reading ability"?

Is "sense of humor" after "sense of responsibility"?

Where is "athletic talent" compared to "poise in social settings"?

Suppose Tom and Carrie both get a "C" in science. Do I congratulate them? Scold them? Congratulate one and scold the other? Was one just sliding by and the other working hard? Am I sure?

It takes time for my children and for me to discover the variety of talents they have been given. Monica and the kids have already figured out that my list has "mechanical ability" almost near the end. Right before "knows how to hang up the towel in the bathroom."

A couple of winters ago the battery in our station wagon croaked during a cold snap. I dug out the jumper cables and hooked them up to our other car and managed to almost drain all the juice out of the good battery, too.

That's pretty much the story of my life when it comes to fixing things.

I tried again a few days later and was able to get the station wagon running. I was glaring at the engine when I felt a pat on the back. It was Tom.

"Way to go, Dad," he said. He meant it. I had the feeling he knew I could do it. Which is more than I knew. Maybe that comes from living with somebody day in and day out. In some ways, you get to know people better than they know themselves.

It always surprises me when one of my kids acts really grown up and gives me a gentle nudge with a word of encouragement or congratulations or consolation.

Tom's words meant a lot to me. He's very gifted when it comes to machines. When he was younger, it bothered me to have him hanging around while I was trying to accomplish some major task. Put new line in the weed whacker, for example. He was always butting in, always pointing at something, always offering a suggestion.

Finally I began to listen to him because, nine times out of ten, he was right and I was wrong.

When we spent time one summer traveling around the country, we were in Wall, South Dakota, when Monica noticed one of our rear tires was in desperate need of more air.

Put air in a tire. Sure. How tough could that be?

Well, it turned out that the hubcap had slid around a little so I couldn't get the air hose on the nozzle.

"You're gonna have to take the hubcap off," the fellow at the self-service gas station said. He was about 105. He disappeared in the back for a minute or two and then returned with a rubber mallet and a huge screwdriver.

"Here," he said, handing them to me.

"Thank you."

I banged around the rim a few times, trying to pry the screwdriver under the edge of it. Then Monica tried. Then I tried again. I presume watching the two of us—the social worker and the writer—was the most entertaining comedy this guy had seen in quite some time.

"Try here," Tom finally said, pointing at a tiny, itsy-bitsy, minuscule, microscopic indentation on the rim. I growled but I did what he had suggested. The tip of the screwdriver fit perfectly and the hubcap popped off.

Tom smiled, pleased that he could help and equally pleased that I was able to get the job done. I hope I give him that same look sometimes when he finishes his homework. School is really hard for him. I hope that sometimes I'm able to point out ways it might be a little easier.

In St. Matthew's Gospel (Mt 25:14-30), Jesus tells the parable about the king who gave five, two, and one talent—amounts of money—to his servants. The first two went out and doubled the king's funds. The third buried it and wanted some praise for not losing anything.

Each of my three children has talents, too. In some areas five, in others two, and in still others only one. I want them to know that in some things they'll be extremely successful and in others they won't do well at all.

They can't compare themselves to each other.

They can't compare themselves to other people. They shouldn't feel smug if they're more talented than some or feel bad if they're less talented than others.

God's given them what they need to use.
They just need to use what God's given them.
So do I.

# EIGHTEEN

# "Take the Kick"

"TAKE THE KICK, ANDY!" the soccer coach yelled from the sideline to my son. It was a Saturday afternoon game and the opposition had made a mistake. The Hawks were going to get a chance to boot it near the goal.

Andy usually plays defense, right in front of the goalie. Maybe being one of the smallest guys on the team and being the youngest member in our family has helped him develop some form of self-defense and taught him how to react quickly. He's able to figure out where the ball is heading and get there first to mess up the other team's offense.

So it was unusual for the coach to tell Andy to move up and take the kick at the other end of the field. He trotted up there, took a few steps back from the ball, came charging forward and tried to send it to another Hawk up closer to the goal. Instead it went to the left.

Way to the left.

Way, way, way to the left.

I yelled, "That's OK" or the equivalent and so did the coach and some of the other parents beside me. It really was. The Hawks were ahead and stayed there.

Later Andy made some really nice defensive plays, but when he came off the field he was shaking his head and muttering about *The Kick*. He said it with capital letters.

The next day we were at one of Carrie's games, and one

girl could really put her foot into the ball. I commented on it to Andy and he answered, "Better than I can."

Then I remembered my own baseball experiences. As a dad, I don't often think of the right thing to say at the right time. This time I got lucky.

"When I played baseball in seventh and eighth grade," I told him, "I used to hit just fine in practice. Then, during a game, the coach would send me up as a pinch hitter and I'd strike out. Every time. I'd go back to practice and hit OK, go up to pinch hit again and strike out."

"I didn't know you played baseball," he said.

"Oh, yeah. Not very well. But I played. Mostly I just sat on the bench. But I had fun."

"Then when did you play basketball?"

"That was when I was a senior in high school."

I didn't add that it was a tiny, tiny school and they needed twelve players because they had twelve uniforms. I remember the day the coach handed them out. He held up the biggest pair of shorts and asked, "Who's got the biggest can?"

Everyone said, "Dodds."

It was great, the way I could bring the team together like that.

"You used to get sent into the game when there were eight seconds left," Andy said. I was surprised—and pleased—he remembered my telling him that.

I considered reminiscing about the time the coach spotted my mom and dad in the crowd and sent me in at the end of the third quarter. I was very concerned. I was afraid he thought the game was almost over, making a mistake like that.

But Andy was already smiling at what a horrible ball player his father was.

"I don't think I ever got a hit during a real game," I said. "And I played two years. And I know I never got a basket in basketball."

He laughed.

That's what I was good at. Even back then. I could make the other players laugh. Sometimes with how I played, but mostly with what I would say. I remember having a lot of fun joking around. Feeling that I was a part of the team. And I was.

Sometimes I make the mistake of only telling my kids stories about myself where I'm the hero. I like to dwell on the ones where I make the right choice or come through in a clutch situation.

Let me tell you about being editor of the yearbook.

About the time I had the lead in the school play.

Yes, my children, before I became Superman, I was Superboy.

Yeah, right.

They prefer hearing about how I screwed up. How I got shafted. How I did something incredibly stupid. They know I did. I still do. They know I'm human so I might as well admit it. It's better if I admit it. Not just for me, but for them. Then they can admit they aren't always the best and the brightest.

They can start to realize they don't have to be a star at something to have fun doing it. They can give it their best shot and just bump along, and sometimes things will work out great and sometimes they're going to really louse it up.

Kind of like the way that I'm a dad. I can't ask them to be perfect. They don't expect me to be.

I don't think God expects perfection either. It's more like he's on the sideline and sometimes—right out of the blue— he yells, "Take the kick!"

I hope my kids will always be willing to trot up the field and give it a shot.

I hope they notice he never demands, "Make a goal!''

# NINETEEN

# Getting Into the Habit

"LET'S GO, TOM! COME ON! HURRY UP, HUH!" I shouted from the hallway through the closed bathroom door. The five of us live in a one-bathroom house, so following a tight morning schedule is part of daily life.

Monica gets up first. Then she wakes Tom. Then I get up. Then Carrie and then Andy. Tom has to be out the front door by 6:58 to catch the school bus a couple of blocks away at 7:07.

"LET'S GO!" I urged him on again—yelled at him again—as he put on his jacket. "GET YOUR BACKPACK! GET YOUR LUNCH! YOU GOTTA MOVE!"

He caught the bus in time and I didn't see him again until after school when I urged (shouted at) him to get started on his homework.

Then it was cleaning his room.

Using proper manners at the dinner table.

Helping with the dishes.

Getting his clothes and backpack ready for the next day of school.

Going to bed.

It wasn't until the next day that it dawned on me that anytime I had spoken to Tom I had been shouting and I sounded mad. That was awful. I bet if someone had asked him to draw a picture of his father Tom would have shown a bullhorn.

At best.

What had happened? Somehow I had turned up the volume and left it there. It hadn't been on purpose. I just slipped into that way of speaking to him. It was . . . just a habit.

Forming a habit isn't necessarily good or bad. What helps or hurts others and myself are the kinds of habits I form. A problem is that I'm not even aware of some of my habits and usually those are the bad kind. The kind I don't want my children to imitate. It's not that people are lazy; it's just that they fall into patterns that become comfortable.

As a dad, I need to remember that my way—my habit— isn't necessarily the only way or even the best way. Take mowing the lawn, for example. I go in a big clockwise circle but Tom goes back and forth in straight rows. Clearly, I am right and he is wrong. Right? Clearly, it does not matter.

I want my kids to know that little things don't count. What matters here is that the job gets done.

But—and maybe this is what makes being a dad such a tricky proposition: there is always at least one "but"—but, I also want my kids to know that little things *do* count.

Getting into the habit of saying please and thank you is a little thing, but an important one. It's a simple and easy way to show respect for others. It says, "You have value. You have worth." It is (I hope I don't sound too grandiose here) a pro-life statement.

Some people have developed a pessimistic attitude and it influences the way they see everything, including themselves. Most often it's nothing more than a series of tiny habits. The weather is too hot or too cold. Or too in between. The restaurant food wasn't quite good enough or served fast enough. The movie at the theater was OK, but the seats were bad. Or the seats were good, but the show stunk. And on and on and on.

It isn't that the glass is half empty and not half full. It's more that the glass has smudges on it, too, and what's in there anyway? Only water? No ice? (Sigh . . .) Oh, well . . .

Habits influence me in so many ways. What do I do when I'm tired, angry, sad, disappointed, happy, worried? What do I want my three kids to do as adults when they experience those same feelings? What do I want them to do now?

I know that the seeds I plant now—a positive approach to the world, self-confidence, the ability to work hard, a trust in God—can bear fruit in them for a long, long time. I know that if my children see those things in me, see that those things are simply a part of my life—habits—then my kids will be more likely to want them in their lives, too.

# TWENTY

# The Best Dreams Can Come True

TOM WAS ABOUT ELEVEN when he started talking about getting his driver's license and buying a Ferrari Testarossa. He had it all figured out.

Except for maybe the money part.

I haven't asked him what color his Ferrari will be. I'm sure he knows. I haven't asked him if he will give me a ride in it. I bet he will. I haven't asked if he will let me drive it. I have my doubts about that.

I suppose he sees himself behind the wheel, tooling down the highway. Zipping over to the store to pick up a gallon of milk for dinner. Dropping his younger brother and sister off at school.

Can three people fit into a Testarossa?

I don't know. I don't know if Tom knows.

Details don't matter when you're daydreaming. When Monica and I talk about someday having "our waterfront home," we don't worry about the beach eroding.

I'm glad Tom has his dream. We've explained to him that the first part of it, the driver's license part, depends on his ability to read. That's not easy for kids like him who live near the border separating "slow learner" and "mildly mentally retarded."

Learning to read is part of the dream that can come true. The part that's more important than any Italian sports car. The same is true for our place on the beach. "Our" is the important part. Without Monica and the kids, without friends and family, it wouldn't be a home, just a house.

I want my kids to dream. To dream big. I don't want them to begin limiting themselves, to become mired down with "I can't."

At the same time, I want them to dream about, to hope for, to work toward, the right stuff. Stuff that has to do with people and skills and developing oneself, not stuff that's centered on possessions or power. I think some of the saddest folks in the world are those who work so hard to provide their families with everything but are never around.

Dad stops being a person and becomes a source of income. He is a stranger in this very beautiful house he works so hard to provide.

There's a danger in chasing the wrong dream, and there's a danger in believing that dreams come true because of luck, in thinking simple wishing can change a life. I suppose some people would say it's luck or fate that two people meet each other and fall in love. I'd say it's God. But it isn't luck that keeps them in love day in and day out, year after year. It isn't luck—wishing or dreaming—that nurtures that relationship, that helps that love grow. It's work.

And God's help.

I always like interviews with professional ball players who say God gave them talent, and they busted their tails developing it. That's how they *made* their dreams come true.

That's how most dreams come true.

Andy and Carrie have dreams, too. They've both figured out what careers they want when they grow up, but I know their decisions may change. I try not to take advantage of it by saying things like "You can't expect to get into medical school with a B in science," or "Professional soccer players don't stay in shape by spending the afternoon playing video games.''

I think for kids, dreams are a lot like playing dress up. You try on a hat, a coat, a pair of shoes. You stand in front of a full-length mirror and turn this way and that. Maybe you keep part of that ensemble on and add a scarf or gloves. Maybe you toss it all and start over from scratch. In either case, you don't need dad butting in, offering unsolicited advice. Not then. That's just a fun time when there are no rules, when there are no limits.

The hard part comes—there's always a hard part—as the kids get older and have to choose. Saying yes to one dream means saying no to many others.

I know that God loves my children more than I do. His love is perfect. Mine often leaves a lot to be desired. He wants them to dream, to imagine what they can do with their lives.

He wants the same for me.

Growing up, getting older, means the end to some things. Some days it seems like the end to a lot of things. But it's not the end of dreaming. I can see myself being a better dad and I can choose to work toward that.

A better husband.

Son.

Brother.

Friend.

Dreams are a sign that I have hope and hope is one of the greatest gifts God gives me. It's one of the greatest gifts I can give my children.

# TWENTY-ONE

# Answering God's Call to Happiness

I WAS FOURTEEN YEARS OLD when my father drove me to St. Edward's Seminary, nestled in the woods in a sleepy little town called Kenmore, about ten miles from our Seattle home. It might as well have been a million.

I was scared, but I wanted to be a priest. I thought God wanted me to be a priest. I thought he was "calling" me. I thought I had a vocation.

I do, of course, but it isn't to the priesthood. I left the seminary six years later, after four years of high school and two years of college. I had spent a weekend home once a month and Christmas, Easter, and summer vacations with my family, but I didn't really move back home until after my sophomore year in college.

That summer I turned twenty, so for almost all of my teenage years I didn't live at home. When I mention that now to my parents they just smile. Now that my own children are hitting that age, those smiles make a lot more sense.

I've asked Tom if maybe he wouldn't like to try a boarding school, but he's not too interested. Especially not in one that's all boys. Where you go to Mass every day. And have to wear a tie to class.

It's a different world now. And a different church. The basic truths are the same, but some of the trimmings have changed almost completely.

I left the seminary to attend the University of Washington. I thought I'd get a degree there and then go down to a seminary in Oakland where my brother was. Instead, I met Monica, fell in love, and got married.

I have come to realize I didn't have a vocation to the priesthood, but I did have a calling to the seminary. It was the right thing to do and the right time to do it. Both the going and the leaving of it. And now I've come to realize my parents made it easy for me to do both. That's what I want to do with my children. I want to have that kind of faith in them and in God.

I remember that ten-mile ride in our '61 blue Falcon and I wonder what Dad was thinking. I was the first of us five kids to leave home. Mary was a high school senior that year, and Mike was a junior. Teresa was in seventh grade, and Betsy was entering fifth. Years later Betsy told me she had mentioned to a classmate that her brother was in the seminary and her friend had gushed condolences. She thought Betsy said "cemetery."

Dad must have taken the morning off work to be able to drive me. Neither one of us knew much about the minor seminary. It was where young men—boys really—went to study to become priests. I remember we talked about the principal, Father Melvin Farrell. His name stood out because Farrell is Mom's maiden name and my middle name.

Fourteen years later, it became Andy's middle name.

Dad and I thought Father Farrell ran the place. We didn't know that rectors, not principals, were in charge. Father Farrell was the first published writer that I ever met. His verses were in our hymnals and his articles were in the weekly magazine the freshman class used for religion class.

Looking back, I can see that he influenced my choice of careers. And my style. His writing was very simple but it got his point across to the reader. I hope mine does the same in the same way. Father died a few years ago, but not before he mentioned to me that I was a case of "the student surpassing the master."

He was very kind.

The other memory I have of Father Farrell is on the football field. I can see him taking the snap, rolling out of the pocket, and letting fly with a bomb way down the field.

I discovered priests—and writers—are human. They're ordinary folks. They are not perfect. I want to teach my kids that no one is perfect, but each person has a lot of goodness in him or her.

Don't put people on pedestals.

But don't put them down either.

Look at them eye-to-eye and realize God created them, God is calling them. They, too, have a vocation. They—like me, like my kids—are stumbling along trying to answer that call.

Sometimes I do a pretty good job responding. Sometimes I put God "on hold." Sometimes I have sense enough to realize the only way I will be truly happy, truly at peace, is to listen to what God wants me to do and then do it.

He wants what is best for me. He is a loving father. And unlike me, he is a perfect father.

If my children listen to him, they will hear him calling. I need to encourage them to do that. I need to show them that I have to do that still. I need to continue to follow my own parents' example, to show that I have faith in God and in my child.

The day after my thirty-sixth birthday I quit my job. I had worked at a diocesan newspaper for ten years, including four years as editor. The paper's policies were shifting, but more than that, I wanted to write full time. Write on my own. It sounds corny but I felt "called" to that. On a good day it seemed like God was nudging me. On a bad, it felt more like nagging.

On the evening of the day I quit, Mom and Dad were out at our house for a birthday celebration. I felt pretty numb, realizing the line between brave and stupid is a very fine one, indeed. Once again, they showed their love, their support, their faith.

I hope, I pray, I can do even half as well with Tom, Carrie, and Andy.

TWENTY-TWO

# Drugs Kill

I WANT MY KIDS TO BE brave and confident, but I don't want them to think they are indestructible. A lot of teenagers die because they think they cannot die. Too many are killed in accidents in which alcohol or some other drug is involved.

Even one death is too many if that young person is someone you loved and someone who loved you.

I want my children to know alcohol is a drug. It's a legal drug if you're twenty-one or older, but it's still a drug. It doesn't matter what form it's in—beer, wine, or the hard stuff—the alcohol is the same. The drug is the same.

Alcohol is a socially acceptable drug, and most people use it moderately as a beverage. Others abuse it. They drink it to relax, to unwind, to calm down. To become numb. To avoid facing reality. To keep on going, even though the direction they're going is down.

I quit drinking alcohol several years ago because it had ceased being a beverage for me and had become a tranquilizer. I didn't lose my family, my job or my house, but I understand how that can happen to people.

Some people are more susceptible to alcohol. More vulnerable. Allergic, if you will. Medical science says that because I am that way, there is a chance that my children will be that way. Carrie and Andy, anyway. Tom, our adopted one, may have lucked out here.

But I'm afraid that, like a lot of dads, I still send a mixed message to my kids. I tell them not to drink and I don't drink, but I still laugh and reminisce about my college exploits. About the time when I was young and thought I was indestructible. When I was young and stupid. When I was lucky that I got to be older and, I hope, a little smarter.

I send a mixed message when I say "don't drink" and then laugh at a TV show with characters who are drunk. When Hawkeye and B.J. and Colonel Potter and the gang are crocked on reruns of "MASH." Would I laugh if they were misusing another drug? If tonight's rerun featured Radar getting wasted on coke?

I don't want to bring back Prohibition, but I want my three kids to know they are going to be bombarded to drink. It isn't just from their friends—"Whatsamatter? You chicken or somethin'?"—it's also from the beer, wine, and hard liquor industry that spend millions and millions each year encouraging people to drink. As the baby-boomer generation gets a little older and slows down in the amount of alcohol it consumes, the industry must now work at attracting new customers. It's a capitalistic fact of life.

It's true that some ads say "drink responsibly." But the first word in that message is still "drink." Famous athletes and media folks have a jolly old time arguing about whether a light beer is best because it tastes great or because it doesn't fill up the drinker. Another brand has created its own equivalent to the Super Bowl.

The commercials are clever and funny and persuasive.

How do I compete with that?

And keep in mind that for anyone twenty-one or older, alcohol is a legal drug.

What about the illegal ones? What about pot and coke? What about crack and ice? Someone is going to talk to my kids about them. Someone who is using them or selling them or both. I firmly believe that there is no spot in this country that is immune. That is safe.

Drugs are everywhere. Wherever you live, there are people who are working hard to sell them. These sellers might be adults in shiny new sports cars, but most likely they are kids about the same ages as my kids. Most likely they are kids who are already hooked and need money to support their own habits. These people will talk to my kids. No matter what I do. No matter how hard I try to protect Tom, Carrie, and Andy.

At first these people will offer my kids drugs at a big, big discount. They may offer my kids a freebie or two.

And I won't be there.

They will be on their own. They are on their own. I sound as if all this is going to happen in the future. It is already happening. I know it has happened. And my child—alone—had to say yes or no.

Tom told Monica and me about it. He told us how he said no. I don't know if I have ever been prouder of him. I hope I told him that right then and there. I hope he heard me say it and remembers it.

The only chance I see for any kids is to arm them with information, the cold, hard facts. To teach them what drugs really are and what drugs really do. To explain that "Don't do drugs" is not on a par with "Wash your hands before you sit down for dinner."

I'm a dad and like all dads, I nag my kids a lot. Sometimes I wish I could rate my nags. "Don't do drugs" would be a number one. Top of the list. Maybe you left the gate to the backyard open and the dog is running down the street. That's not good. It is nothing—NOTHING!—compared to using drugs.

Some authorities say it's possible for a person to become addicted to crack cocaine after only one use.

One use.

A dare. An experiment. Curiosity. A simple act of rebellion.

One.

It's like playing Russian roulette with a gun that's fully loaded.

Tom and Carrie have both been through the D.A.R.E. (Drug Abuse Resistance Education) program at their school. It's a good one. Carrie's instructor said he believed all the police forces in the country could double in size and still not stop the problem. His words meant more because he's a cop. "Education is the key," he told the students and their parents.

Drugs are a plague and I pray that my house, that my loved ones, are spared. And I pray for the kids who have died. For those who are going to die.

# TWENTY-THREE

# "That's Not Fair!"

THERE'S AN OLD SAYING that "all's fair in love and war." Like most dads, I've discovered nothing's fair when it comes to kids.

It is impossible to make life fair for my three children, no matter how hard I try. Maybe, like a lot of parents, sometimes I'm trying too hard.

When Tom, Carrie, or Andy say to me, "That's not fair!"—although they seldom say it and often mutter, hiss, or shout it—I am very tempted to reply, "Duhhhhh!"

But since I do not let them answer that way to each other when one of them says something very stupid, I cannot do it either. Pity.

I don't know where my children got the idea that life is supposed to be fair. Or that it ever will be fair. Or that a parent can ever make it fair.

I don't want to show favoritism to one of my kids. I don't want to give them the idea that I love one more than the other two. I don't. Parents often say "I love you equally" and children doubt it. They think that's impossible. But it can be done. A dad can love his kids so much that it really can't be measured or compared.

Christmas can be a classic time for inequality. What if Tom wants a remote control airplane and Andy wants a foam football? Then it's pretty obvious that because one item costs hundreds of dollars and one costs five bucks, Andy is much more likely to have his wish come true. But maybe not. Maybe Mom and Dad are going to come up short on that one, too.

That was the case one year. He asked for a special "turbo" football with twists in it to enable anyone—a young boy, for example—to toss a fifty-yard pass. Or so he said. (Carrie had a different opinion: "Not if you've got a wienie arm to start with." Merry Christmas.)

Monica and I went to more than a half dozen stores and couldn't find the football. I suppose we looked so diligently because it was a cheap request. And—foolish us—we thought it was an easy one, one we could meet.

We did meet a lot of parents in toy departments staring at empty shelves where *The Football* was supposed to be. Before some lucky mom or dad scooped up the last one.

Andy didn't get the ball. He survived. But he knew that there were thousands of kids all over the country who were spending Christmas afternoon throwing their new turbo footballs. He knew every pass went at least half the length of a football field.

That isn't fair! Why did they get one when he didn't! Right. It isn't fair, but carry that thought just a little bit farther. Why are there so many children in this country who get nothing? Why do so many live in poverty? Why do so many live in homes where they are abused? Why do so many face conditions daily that would easily crush the strength and spirit of just about any adult?

That's not fair.

I want my children to know this. And that's only in this country, a land so very, very wealthy compared to the rest of the world.

My children do not wonder if they will eat today.

If they will be warm.

If they will have a place to sleep.

God has blessed them—and me—with so many material

goods. Like so many of the stories in the Gospels, there are two versions to the Beatitudes. In Matthew, Jesus says, "Blessed are the poor in spirit" (Mt 5:3). In Luke, it's "Blessed are you who are poor" (Lk 6:20).

St. Matthew's version is a lot easier to take than St. Luke's. I don't believe God expects me to be destitute, but I have to draw the line between "need" and "want." Between "necessity" and "luxury." I don't want my children to be beggars. I don't want them to be a couple of princes and a princess either.

When I was working as a newspaper reporter, I would sometimes interview new arrivals to the United States. Refugees from Asia or Eastern Europe or Central or South America would talk about conditions in their native countries. In the evening, safe and snug in my little three-bedroom ranch house in the suburbs, I would feel secure.

I would feel extremely rich.

Sometimes, when money seemed especially tight, I would—half kidding—suggest to the paper's photographer that we should find a refugee to interview. It would help me realize again that life isn't fair and that I'm way over on the rich side.

I think there is another area where that phrase is used a lot. It's when it comes to sickness, to disabilities, and to death. Why are some people mentally retarded? Why are some bedridden or confined to a wheelchair? Why do some die so young, under tragic circumstances?

It isn't fair.

Why would God allow this?

Why isn't God fair?

A couple of years ago I was interviewing people for an article on chronic pain. How do people cope with that day in and day out, and why does God allow it? I was talking about it with my big brother—the priest/theologian/college professor. "I wrote about that in my doctoral dissertation," he said.

"Yeah? So what's the answer?"

He smiled. "It's a mystery."

He didn't mean that "The Unchanging God of Love: A Study of the Teaching of St. Thomas Aquinas on Divine Immutability in View of Certain Contemporary Criticism of This Doctrine" is a script for "Murder, She Wrote." He meant that why God allows this pain is something we can't understand.

The church teaches that our suffering can somehow be joined to the suffering that Christ endured on Calvary, that it has value, and can become a source of grace. But the why . . . the why is a question that continues to be asked.

St. Paul wrote something that helps me in this area. In 1 Corinthians 13, right after he talks about love, he says that now we see only a dim reflection in a mirror, but someday we'll see clearly. Someday we'll see "face to face" and then we'll understand.

I don't think mirrors back then worked as well as mirrors do today. More like a dim reflection in a muddy puddle. I can make out shape and movement, but the details just aren't there.

Don't worry about the mystery, I need to tell my kids. You won't understand it. No human has. But keep in mind another saying: "Of those to whom much has been given, much is expected."

They should be able to understand that one. After all, it's only fair.

# TWENTY-FOUR

# Trust: Fragile, Handle with Care

"IT WASN'T SO MUCH THAT I WAS MAD AT HER, but I was so disappointed," a friend and fellow parent was saying to me. "She just didn't realize what she had done. I didn't know if I could trust her anymore."

His daughter was a sixth-grader and a good student, but she had been caught cheating on a test. Not a big test, her dad explained to me, but it was one she hadn't studied for and she panicked, and had some notes scribbled on a tiny sheet of paper. Her social studies teacher caught her dead-bang.

"I guess I should be glad about that," he said. "I mean, that she's a good student and a bad cheater."

I smiled.

"She says she never did it before but now . . ." His voice trailed off.

I knew what he hadn't said: "Now I don't know if I can believe her."

That's a tough place for a parent to be. Monica and I have been there. Every parent has. I could come up with examples from our family life, but I don't want to embarrass the kids.

I could come up with examples from my own past.

That father was right. Cheating was a dumb idea, but it

wasn't really a big deal. She got caught. She got an F on that test. It brought her average down a little bit.

I'm sorry.

You're forgiven.

End of story.

Not quite.

"It upsets her that her teacher seems to be hovering around her desk more now," the dad said. " 'It's like she's spying on me,' my daughter said. I told her the teacher just wants to make sure she isn't cheating again. 'I'm not,' my daughter said. 'I won't.'

" 'But how does your teacher know that?' I asked her. 'Because I said so.' So I told her that right now that wasn't good enough. The old 'your actions speak louder than your words' is really true. 'You have to earn back her trust,' I said. 'And that takes time.' "

That's a tough lesson for any child, but maybe especially for one living in the "instant" age. Instant breakfast, instant potatoes, instant microwave meals. You want to watch a TV show or movie when you want to and not when the television station broadcasts it? Just tape it. And fast forward through the commercials. Waiting is for fools.

And fathers stuck in rush-hour traffic.

Now she was learning that trust is a very delicate commodity. It takes a long time to establish it and one foolish act to wipe out most, if not all, of it. Now she was discovering there is no way to instantly repair that damage. It takes time and no one can say just how long.

I used to be director of the Search program for the Archdiocese of Seattle. My job was to help organize and direct weekend retreats for juniors and seniors in high school.

I was much younger then.

One of the exercises that we did was called a "trust walk." The kids would pair up and go out for a walk. But one would have his or her eyes closed. The non-seeing person had to depend on a partner's directions. Then they would reverse roles. It was a popular exercise and not just because it was a good excuse for a boy or girl to go out walking hand-in-hand. (Although that was part of it, of course.)

After everybody was back in the meeting room, we'd talk about what it had been like. Some of the teens liked leading and admitted they couldn't keep their eyes closed when they were being led. Others preferred to be led and didn't like having the responsibility of making sure a partner didn't get hurt.

That simple game was a good lead-in to talking about faith, about where we put our trust and why. What would happen if your partner was a joker and had you stepping up or down from "curbs" that weren't there or walking into bushes? How many times could he do that before you didn't believe what he was saying?

What happens if a friend tells you something in confidence and you don't keep it secret?

What happens if you get a reputation for borrowing stuff and not returning it?

What happens if you promise your parents you'll do something and then you "forget" or simply back out on the deal?

Now for me, that last question can be reversed: What happens if I promise my kids something and then change my mind? What's that teaching them? Why should they trust me when I promise something again? Aren't my actions speaking louder than my words?

I want my children to trust me, even though there will be times when I fall short. More than that I want them to follow the advice offered on United States coins: "In God we trust." That, when you think about it, is a funny place to have that message, considering how many people have more faith in money than they do in God.

They might not say that. They probably wouldn't. But again, how do they act? If they spend their lives chasing money or fame or power, if they think science or technology has all the answers, where is their faith? Literally, what do they believe in? Where do they place their confidence?

When I fall into those traps—and it's so easy to do—where am I putting my trust?

Jesus said that if a person has faith—has trust in God—the size of a mustard seed, a little bitty thing, then he or she could move mountains. Many people have that kind of faith, they really believe what God has revealed and what the church teaches. I've met some of them and they have a happiness, a peace, money can't buy. They aren't hemmed in by the mountains of doubt and worry that seem to surround this dad—sometimes.

# TWENTY-FIVE

# Are Heaven and Hell
# for Real?

"I JUST NEED TO SIT DOWN FOR A MINUTE," the photographer said.

"Let me get you a chair," the nurse immediately answered.

"Oh, no. This is fine," the photographer replied. "I'll just sit here." Her legs folded up and she plopped down on the floor. She looked white. Very white.

"I'll get you a drink of water," the nurse said and the photographer nodded. After she was feeling better, she seemed a little embarrassed. I assured her it was all right. We had covered a lot of stories together and she hadn't made fun of me when I got air sick in the single-engine plane. That was during the interview of the guy who did traffic reports on the radio.

The story we were working on that morning was overwhelming: the burn unit in a local hospital. The nurse had explained the procedures a patient must endure and we had met some people who had been hurt.

I couldn't imagine a more devastating or painful injury. I still can't.

Monica remembers my working on that story. She says that evening, when I got home, I immediately checked the labels in the kids' pajamas to make sure they were made of flame retardant material.

I remember telling my editor about the interview and tour. Later she told me that right after our conversation she phoned home to make sure the coffee pot wasn't too close to the edge of the counter where her preschooler might accidentally pull it down on himself.

That burn unit made it easy to understand why fire has been used for so long to describe hell. It's a good description. I don't mean hell is so many degrees Fahrenheit. I mean a person is able to injure himself—maim himself—to that degree spiritually. He can turn and run that far from all that's good. He can turn and run that far from God.

I believe hell is a reality, but it's very difficult for me to explain it to my kids because I don't understand it. I believe it exists the same that I believe evil exists. When we say the "Our Father" at Mass—the prayer Christ taught his followers to pray—we ask God to "deliver us from evil."

I can't tell Tom, Carrie, and Andy that hell is some kind of a sauna with the thermostat gone haywire, filled with devils in red satin suits. It's not a home for nasty little folks who have horns and tails and carry pitchforks. I don't think those cartoon characters capture the awful reality of evil.

I want my kids to know they can't stand still. Spiritually, I mean. They are either moving toward God or away from him. The farther away they get from him, the closer they are to hell. To a certain extent, the more they are already experiencing some of the pains of hell.

The pains of being separated from the source of life.

The closer they get to God, the closer they are to heaven. The more they are enjoying the kingdom of God, a kingdom that can begin right here, right now, for anyone who chooses it.

Jesus used some easy-to-understand terms when he described the kingdom of heaven. In St. Matthew's Gospel (chapter 13), he says it's like a mustard seed. It's extremely tiny but can grow to a huge shrub that becomes a home for birds. It's like yeast that can transform flour. It's like a treasure buried in a field. If someone finds it, he sells everything to buy that piece of land.

But I can't explain heaven anymore than I can explain hell. One is being completely with God; one is being completely without him. I can't imagine either.

What I can tell my children is that there is more to life than what they will experience here. They will live forever. Those who die in Christ will rise to eternal life.

But how can there be a hell? Eternal death. Why would God allow it?

God has given me free will. I can choose what I do today. What I'll do tomorrow. What I'll do with my life. With each choice I move closer to God or farther away from him. I will be happier, more at peace, more human—more the being God created me to be—if I choose to do his will. Simply, if I choose to love God and do good.

I hope my kids know that doing good isn't earth-shaking or complicated. It's nothing more than making a simple decision and acting on it.

Maybe it's too simple. Maybe that's why it's hard to see life that way. To believe these seemingly insignificant actions can mean so much.

# TWENTY-SIX

# Discipline Is Good for a Child

"**D**ISCIPLINE IS GOOD FOR A CHILD."

My three kids have heard me say that a lot of times over the years. Now wait a minute, that's not quite right. I've said it to my three kids many times over the years. I have no idea how many times they actually listened to me.

It could be they had tuned me out by the time I came up with one of my favorite proverbs. I usually remind them of the fact right before or right after I tell them they have to do something they don't want to do.

But then, that's what discipline is all about. It's the ability to do something when you don't want to do it. It can be as simple—simple?—as getting up in the morning when the alarm goes off.

But as every dad knows—"Dad the Disciplinarian"—it also can mean being the arresting officer, prosecuting attorney, judge, jail guard, and parole board member. When Tom, Carrie, and Andy were little, that system of justice and education sometimes included a swat to the rear end. The object was not to cause pain, but to put an exclamation point on the message being delivered.

"If your ball goes out into the street, you do not just run right out after it! Never! Ever!"

As they got older, calling for a time out" proved the most effective. (Has proven the most effective. Monica and I aren't out of the woods yet. Not by a long shot.) The ultimate sentence is going to bed early or sitting on a dining room chair and doing absolutely nothing for five, ten, or fifteen minutes. Then, too, there are various forms of "grounding." A bit like having one of them under house arrest.

And, of course, I yell. My yelling used to be a lot more effective. When I went off to work every day and the kids didn't see me too often, my yelling worked a lot better. Now that I work at home, they see me all the time. They hear me all the time. I have to settle a lot more disputes. That's a nice way of saying "pull the combatants away from each other." So now the kids have grown accustomed to my screaming voice. Sometimes it seems that they don't even notice me. It's a lot like people who live near a major airport who don't seem to notice the roar of the jets.

On some days any dad can match a jet, decibel for decibel.

Crime and punishment are part of discipline: "You break the rule, you pay the price." But it's a lot more than that. A lot harder than that. Self-discipline is what I want for my kids.

It's what I want for me, too.

That means saying no. I know some parents are afraid to say that to their kids. They're afraid it will traumatize them or discourage them or stunt them in some way.

Part of my being a loving father, though, is saying no. Saying it clearly and firmly. Part of my being a loving father is teaching my children that they can't have everything they want right when they want it. Sometimes, they can't have it at all.

That's what they're going to experience when they are on their own. When they are grown and on the job, when they are parents, when they need to function as members in society, they are going to hear no from others and they are going to need to say no to themselves.

No, I can't afford to spend my paycheck on a really cool color TV with a remote. I need to spend it on rent, food, health insurance, and other really boring stuff.

No, I can't be late for my job day after day, or very soon I won't have any job at all.

No, I can't tell my infant child, "I'm really tired so you can't be sick or hungry or need my attention right now."

I know discipline makes more sense to Tom, Carrie, and Andy when it's called something else: practice. Twice a week during the fall Andy and Carrie have soccer practice. They come home sweaty and dirty and tired and better prepared for the league games they play on the weekend. Once a week Tom has bowling practice with the other members of his team. Some Saturdays he would rather stay home and play video games or go outside and ride his bike or just loaf, but he doesn't. He continues to prepare for upcoming tournaments.

Self-discipline is saying no to a lot of little things because you've said yes to something big. Self-discipline is a thousand halting steps toward a goal that sometimes seems unreachable yet gets closer all the time.

I want my kids to learn that self-discipline—saying no, taking those little steps—brings more than that final goal. It brings a sense of pride, a sense of accomplishment, a sense of satisfaction that can't be experienced any other way.

A Super Bowl ring isn't a piece of jewelry. It's a symbol of years and years and years of hard work.

The ability to play the piano at Carnegie Hall doesn't come by magic or by wishing. It represents hours and hours and hours of sitting in front of the keyboard.

I doubt that my kids will ever wear Super Bowl rings (sorry, Andy) or play at Carnegie Hall. But I want them to have good friendships, to have good marriages (if God is calling them to that vocation and, if not, to be good at the one to which he is calling them), to have good careers. I want them to be good parents, to continue to be good sons and a good daughter. I want them to be good Catholics.

I want them to be good at praying. Good at loving. Good at living.

I believe all those things take discipline.

No matter how old we are, we are the sons and daughters of God. No matter how old we are, discipline is good for a child.

# TWENTY-SEVEN

# The Best Gifts Never End Up in a Sock Drawer

W HEN I WAS A KID my mother said her favorite gifts were the ones we made for her ourselves.

Right, Mom.

I couldn't imagine that. A person would prefer some crummy art project over an item that was new, shiny, and store-bought? Get real. I figured she was just being nice. Moms are supposed to be nice, after all. She knew I didn't have a lot of money for Christmas or her birthday or Mother's Day because I had spent it on important things like model cars or baseball cards or cherry Cokes.

I soon discovered just about every gift you give your dad ends up in his sock drawer. He says, "Oh, yeah, thanks" and then tucks it away next to his hankies. So, being a dutiful son, I tried to get him small things. Now, having kids myself, I wonder if he laughed every morning as he reached for his socks.

Kids—God love them—give the dumbest presents. I have received more useless, impractical, schlocky gifts from Tom, Carrie, and Andy than would seem possible. Unless, of course, you're a dad and then you probably have a similar stash.

Maybe this sounds extremely negative and I don't mean it

107

that way. I have discovered "useless" can also be "price-less." I don't give away or toss away the presents my three give to me. There's no way I could do that.

I think part of the charm of each gift was the fact that the giver thought about what I might want to have.

What does Daddy do?

What does Daddy like?

These days, more often than not, chocolate is involved. They know I have a sweet tooth and, I suspect, they've discovered I'm likely to share the gift with the giver. I remember when they were little, how they sometimes would immediately give back a part of something I had given them. If they received a little bowl of corn chips, they would reach in and take one and offer it.

It always amused me. There I was standing with the bag of chips in my hand and there they were with just a few. But they wanted to share their good fortune with me.

Sometimes I wonder if God feels that way. I hope I show that same spirit of generosity with all the gifts he's given me.

Over the years I've received my share of handmade gifts, too. I've discovered my mother was right. The primitive drawings ("No, Daddy, it's not a house. It's a horse."), the glue-heavy art projects ("We didn't eat all those Popsicles. The teacher had a box of sticks."), and the creative writing ("Is that how you spell 'stupid brother'?") are treasures.

I know I had a part in giving Carrie and Andy life and in giving Tom a home and family, but that can't compare with what they've given me. They gave me a life. They made me a dad.

I like to take a walk after dinner. Monica presumes it's because it's the healthy thing to do. OK. But it also means I'm out of the house while the kids tackle the dinner dishes. And each other. One fall evening Tom grabbed his coat as I was heading for the door and asked if he could go with me.

"Don't you have work to do?" I asked.

"He's 'dry and put away,'" Monica said, describing his

job that evening, "so there's no rush."

So off we went into the cold, dark night. I asked "How's school?" and he answered, "Fine." Pretty typical father-child stuff. We passed a house that was next to a convenience store. The store's sign shone brightly, illuminating the whole area.

That would be awful, I thought. Having that light going all night right outside your bedroom.

"Bright light," Tom said.

"Uh, huh," I agreed, getting ready to make my "that would be awful" observation.

"That'd be great," he said. "Lights up the whole back yard. You could play all night."

Play all night. I remember wanting to do that. When you'd go out after supper and your cheeks and hands kept getting colder and colder and it kept getting harder and harder to see the football or the basketball that some other kid was tossing your way. Finally, somebody's mom or dad would holler it was time to come in. Then it seemed like every other mom and dad on the block had heard the first call and pretty soon everyone had to go.

You'd go back inside and it would seem so hot in there and so bright. Then it was time to start getting ready for bed and, shoot, the day was over.

Tom and I didn't talk about much the rest of the way home that evening. But when we got back inside, the house seemed hotter than usual and the lights seemed brighter and I felt a little sad that this day was ending.

That's what my kids can do for me. That's the gift of "life" they share. They can take an ordinary event and change it. They have taken my humdrum life and changed it. They aren't even aware they've done that, aware that they continue to do that.

The best gifts they give can't be tied up with a bow. The best gifts will never end up in my sock drawer.

God has given them—and me—some pretty incredible

gifts, too. The Father sent his Son. The Son gave his life. The Father and Son sent the Spirit. I believe that because I have the gift of faith. I think my kids have received that gift, too. I pray that they'll always have it.

# TWENTY-EIGHT

# Trying to Live Up to a Label

A DAD USED TO BE ABLE TO ADVISE his kids: "Don't buy some article of clothing just because it has a big-time label. You're paying a lot of extra money for that scrap of cloth and nobody is going to see it. Unless you go around with your clothes inside out."

Har, har, har.

Now my children do go around with their clothes inside out. When they were toddlers and preschoolers, I was able to stop them from doing that. Each hit a point where it was very important to get dressed by him or herself and Monica and I would offer helpful suggestions like "Look for the label. It goes on the inside. In the back."

By the time they got a little older, clothing and shoe manufacturers had discovered people would wear items with the brand name plastered in HUGE letters on the outside. People—my kids, my wife, myself—have become mini-billboards.

One evening we were having spaghetti for dinner and then the kids and I were going out to a grade school gym to shoot hoops. Carrie and Andy both managed to get more than a little tomato sauce on the fronts of their sweatshirts.

"No problem," Carrie said at the end of the meal. She

pulled off the outer shirt—which she had been wearing inside out—and showed that the one underneath was still spotless. Then she turned the sweatshirt right-side out and put it back on. She looked pretty smug.

Andy made the same switch but his sweatshirt went from right-side out to inside out.

My kids do that in a lot of different ways and so do I. Their classmates and teachers and friends and mother and father tend to put labels on them. Sometimes my son or daughter wears one proudly. Like a name brand in letters a foot high on the front of a T-shirt. But sometimes he or she doesn't want anything to do with it.

It becomes a self-fulfilling prophecy. A pigeonhole. A trap which seems inescapable.

"You're funny."

"You're smart."

"You're hard working."

"You're always cheerful."

Those don't sound so bad. Pretty good, in fact. But a person is more than just one of those things. And no one is always funny or smart or hard working or cheerful.

And then there are the other labels.

"You never get your homework done."

"You always fight when it's your turn to wash the dishes."

"One time, why can't you just do what you're told without making some sarcastic remark?"

People are going to label my kids all their lives, but I don't want the three of them to feel trapped by those labels. I want them to be able to flip that sweatshirt inside out or throw it in the hamper or simply toss it out. I want them to be able to say to themselves, "No, that's not me." Or, "Yes, that's a part of me but only a part."

People have always labeled others. Jesus' time was no exception. You are a Jew. You are a Samaritan. You are a Pharisee. You are a tax collector.

He dines with sinners and prostitutes! They're his friends. Those are the kinds of people following *this* fellow.

'Nuff said.

Jesus could look beneath the label. He tried to help others do the same. "Let me tell you a story about a Samaritan," he said (Lk 10:29-37).

"A Samaritan? Great! Have you heard this one? How many Samaritans does it take to . . ."

"A good Samaritan."

"A good one! Get out of here! Really?"

Or another time (Lk 18:9-14), "Let me tell you about a Pharisee and a tax collector who went up to the temple to pray." Pharisees were mucky-mucks. Tax collectors were . . . tax collectors. But in Jesus' story the Pharisee is so pompous God doesn't listen to his words. His prayer is "Thank God I'm better than everyone else." If that can be called a prayer.

The tax collector says to God, "I blew it. I'm sorry."

So—flip those labels—the "good" guy condemns himself and the "bad" guy goes home justified.

As a dad, I'm not too concerned about name-brand clothing. We can't afford it. I am concerned about name-brand kids. I can't afford to let my sons and daughter fall into the trap of letting others define who they are. God has made each of them a unique, multifaceted individual who is more than a string of labels. Each is an ever-changing and growing reflection of a God who created him or her in his own image. A God who is more than all the labels used to describe him, a God who is infinite love.

# TWENTY-NINE

# Prayer and the Holy Spirit

I MUST HAVE BEEN ABOUT NINE YEARS OLD when Dad took me to the Easter midnight Mass. Our parish was St. Cecilia Cathedral in Omaha, Nebraska, and I had no idea the Easter vigil Mass would go on . . . and on . . . and on.

An ordinary Sunday Mass is long when you're nine.

Midnight Mass on Easter seemed to take forever. I must have fallen asleep right after the Gospel. That's as much as I remember. I do recall having said six rosaries by then. I'm not claiming I said them fervently. For all I know, I may have set an indoor speed record.

I don't remember who taught me my prayers. The Hail Mary, the Our Father, the prayer to my guardian angel and so on. I would bet it was Mom. Just because she was around more and usually that's the way it works in a family. The nuts-and-bolts of religion are passed on by a mother.

But then a child looks at his dad and asks: Is this for real or is this like "kiss a boo-boo and make it all better" and the sand man? Is this just cute stuff for little kids?

I think Dad answered that for me at that Easter Mass. Before I nodded off. We all went to Mass every Sunday but that's the only time I can recall that it was just the two of us. I think that's why that night stands out in my memory.

Dad was saying, "Yes, we pray. Yes, I pray." He didn't say it out loud, but the message I got was: praying isn't like hopscotch or jacks or paper dolls. Praying isn't just for girls and for moms. Praying is for guys, too. Even "really old guys" like your father.

I think my own kids look at me that way now. They ask questions without using any words.

What about this safety stuff Mom preaches—bike helmets and fire drills at home and such?

What about this "homework is important" jazz?

What about this eating well-balanced meals?

What about this going to Mass on Sunday?

What about this praying? Is this for real or what?

Oh, yeah. Praying is for real. And there's no substitute.

I want my children to know the standard Catholic prayers that I learned. Partly because those prayers are good ones. They've stood the test of time. And partly because many of them have a distinctive Catholic flavor that's part of their religious cultural background. But also because I know there will be times when they are worried or frightened out of their wits and they will be reaching for the comfort and security of a prayer. They will want to talk to God, and their own words will fail them.

I want them to pray informally, too. To use their own words and talk to their Creator and to Mary and the saints. Sometimes they will be asking for favors. Sometimes they will be saying thank you. Sometimes they will be trying to hear what God has to say to them. And sometimes—I hope a lot of the time—they will simply be enjoying God's company. Words won't be necessary. Not even in their own heads.

I hope they become that comfortable, that at ease, with praying, with being with God. I hope they feel the same way I do when I'm driving the car and one of them is in the front seat beside me. The radio is off and we aren't talking, but the silence isn't awkward. I hope they want to be with God that way. I hope they come to realize God is always with them.

I pray for my kids. I think every dad does. Every dad

wants what's best for his sons and daughters. Trying to figure out what that is isn't always easy.

When Tom, Carrie, and Andy were really little I used to pray that they would be happy, healthy, and know that God loves them. That's still my prayer for them. I want each to have a good life and I know a life filled with prayer is good.

So that's what I ask from God. Over and over again. I nag him about that. Jesus talked about nagging. And dads. In St. Matthew's Gospel (7:7-11) Jesus says, "Go ahead and ask God." He says if you ask, you're going to receive. Keep looking because you're going to find what you want. Keep banging away on that door because someday it's going to open.

Then he talks about dads. He asks if any father is going to hand his son a rock when he asked for a piece of bread. Or a snake when he asked for a fish. Or a scorpion when he asked for an egg. Ridiculous, right? Of course, it is. But, Jesus goes on to say, if fathers here on earth—fathers who are a long, long way from perfect—know how to give their kids what's good, then you can bet that God the Father is going to give good things to those who ask.

And there is nothing better than the Holy Spirit.

I pray that the Holy Spirit will fill my three children and be with them all their lives. I pray that the Holy Spirit will give them the desire to pray and the ability to pray. I pray that I'm doing something—but I don't know what—that is showing Tom, Carrie, and Andy that praying is important. It's not a luxury. It's a necessity. It is a source of strength and courage, knowledge and wisdom, happiness and peace—a source of the Holy Spirit—that can be theirs for the asking.

*Part Three*

# *Special Times Together*

# THIRTY

# Thanksgiving: A Time for Instant Traditions

I T HAS BECOME A THANKSGIVING TRADITION around here that Tom makes his yam dish. He picked up the recipe in school a few years ago and since it includes brown sugar and marshmallows, it's become one of his favorites.

It might more accurately be called his brown sugar and marshmallow dish that has a yam or two in it. Since Carrie and Andy hate it and refuse to eat anything more than their mandatory "small spoonful," Tom likes it even more.

It always amazes me how easy it is to start a family tradition. One Thanksgiving we ate dinner in the early afternoon and then went to a theater to see the latest Disney movie. The next year Andy remarked, "We always go to a movie on Thanksgiving!" So we made plans to try it again.

That first year it was a typical Disney show, but even more entertaining than the movie was the family directly behind us. The four or five kids were older teenagers. But they trooped right in with their parents, anxious to see the show and obviously having a great Thanksgiving. The kind they had probably had since they were peewees.

I don't know if later they told their friends how they had spent Thanksgiving afternoon. It's hard to imagine one of those big guys commenting to his buddies, "Yeah, I saw

'Oliver and Company' and it was really good.'' On the other hand, it's very easy to picture him in about ten or fifteen years, taking his wife and kids to a holiday movie.

I always smile when I hear about young adults—who claim to be so open-minded and liberal—who make such a fuss when somebody tampers with a family tradition.

"But we always have dinner at five."

"We always have Grandma's pie for dessert."

"Mom always makes her special dressing."

"We always watch the football game together."

"We always take a walk after dinner."

Well, "always" had to start somewhere and one of the true joys of being a dad is helping to establish some of those traditions. In recent years, one of our Thanksgiving "always" has been buying pistachio nuts. I have no idea how that one began. But it's the only time of the year that we have them, and they have become a holiday treat.

Society may keep trying to tell my kids that Thanksgiving is a day for food and televised football, but I hope they realize that first it is a time for prayer and a time for family.

Sometimes it's easier for Tom, Carrie, and Andy to say thank you to God than it is for them to say it to each other. Most of the time, I bet. When I insist they say thanks, they can make it sound as insincere as some of the times they're forced to say "sorry."

Giving thanks—like asking forgiveness—can't really be forced. It's one of those intangibles that has to come from within. I feel like I never really thanked my parents until I had children of my own. I'm sure I said thank you to them lots of times, but I didn't realize all they had given me and at what cost.

Not just financial.

Now simply saying thanks to them doesn't seem like enough. I believe the best way to show my appreciation is to be a good parent to my own children. I can't repay Mom and Dad, but I can take what they gave me and pass it on to the next generation. It would show that I appreciate so much what they gave me that I want my own children to have it.

A lot of parishes, including ours, have made Thanksgiving a day to bring food to church for local food banks. That kind of action, that kind of tradition, is really going back to the roots of the holiday.

When my children think about Thanksgiving, I would like them to remember that we went to Mass.

"But it isn't Sunday!" they have a tendency to complain.

No, it's Thursday.

"And it isn't a holy day of obligation, is it?"

Nope.

"Then why do we . . . ?"

Even now Monica answers: "Because it's the right thing to do and we want to thank God for all he's given us, and because we always go to Mass on Thanksgiving."

End of discussion.

It's hard to think of a better way to say thank you. I could tell them that, in fact, the English word "eucharist" is based on the Greek word *eukharistos* which means "grateful."

Maybe I'll do that next November. Maybe I'll make it a Thanksgiving tradition.

# THIRTY-ONE

# My Christmas Wish List

I CHECKED OVER MY CHRISTMAS wish list and figured I didn't stand much of a chance of affording any of it. When I was a kid, the list mentioned the things I wanted to receive. Now, it's more often things I want to give.

Andy would get a computer. One that could play games.

Carrie would get a piano and lessons.

Tom would get a remote control airplane or helicopter. It seemed more likely to me that the airplane would crash into trees. I don't know why it seemed more likely since I didn't know much of anything about either toy except Tom wanted one or the other. Then again, this was a wish list, so I decided to go with the plane.

And for Monica . . .

Monica would get a new house. A bigger house. With two full bathrooms and a large dining room. And a closet in our bedroom. Not a "wardrobe box" made out of plywood by some fool husband who is not very good at making wardrobe boxes out of plywood.

Sometimes the hardest part about being a husband and dad isn't giving up stuff, it's not being able to give your wife and your children all the things you'd like to give them. And then, again, sometimes you're able to give them at least part of it and it feels so good.

That Christmas there was no new home, no remote

control airplane, no piano. But there was a computer. Not a new one. A used one. Bought through the want ads. A real deal. The same make and model that I use in my office and that the kids kept hounding me to get a turn to use.

Most of the time—almost all the time—I'd tell them no. If it got broken, if I had to take it into the shop and leave it there for a couple of weeks, I would be in big, big trouble.

I brought the "new" one out into the living room on Christmas morning and waited for them to start gushing their thanks and surprise.

They didn't gush.

Then I realized what the problem was. "Come here," I said and headed for my office. They followed me. "Look," I said, pointing to my computer. "The one in the living room is for you three," I said. But by then they were gone.

Not gushing. Fighting over who got to go first.

"This is for you and for Mom and me, too," I tracked them down and told them. "Sometimes she has to work on stuff at the same time I do."

"Uh, huh," they answered.

"And if something happened to mine, I would need to use this one, too."

Now it seems to me they said OK. Not "we'll see." Or "Oh, so now suddenly you want to share?"

I don't know if they were distracted over the battle for "I'm first" or caught up in the Christmas spirit. It's easy to get distracted at this time of the year. It's easy to miss the spirit. I hope I'm teaching my kids, showing my kids, that Christmas is Jesus and family and then gifts. I hope I'm making it clear to them that wish lists are fun, but God has already given the greatest gift possible.

One we all can share.

One we don't have to fight over.

One that allows everyone to "be first."

But the gift of his Son—sent to save the world, sent to show the world how to live—isn't free. There's a price tag. If

I hear about this Jesus, about his life and death and resurrection, and I want to believe in him, then I have to show it by how I act.

Not just what I say. What I do.

Not just how I treat my family and friends. How I treat people I don't even like. People who don't like me.

I want Tom, Carrie, and Andy to know that the Christmas message is one of hope and love. Hope for the world. (Not: "I hope I get what I asked for. I know I'd really love it.") But what does that mean? The world is so big and has so many people. Hope for all, but also hope for each of my children. I need to tell them, you can have hope because God loves you this much. God sent his Son—his only child—to earth for you.

This God—who is very famous, by the way, who is featured in books and movies and TV shows—loves you. The God who created the first humans. Who spoke to Abraham. Who led Moses. Who inspired David, Isaiah, and John the Baptist. This God—this same being—sent his Son for you.

To you.

Because of you.

This Father—who is goodness, who is love—made his wish list. It said, "Tom, Jesus. Carrie, Jesus. Andy, Jesus."

On that Christmas, the first Christmas, God gave the perfect gift. One size fits all. Satisfaction guaranteed. No assembly required.

I want my children to know that there could be Christmas without a tree, without stockings, without a big dinner, without all the other trappings.

One gift—the best gift, the only important gift—will always be there. "Here's my Son," God says to them. "Just for you."

# THIRTY-TWO

# The First Day of School

E ACH SEPTEMBER my mother used to take a picture of the five of us on the first day of school. I didn't know why. Maybe because we were wearing new clothes. Maybe because she had survived the summer. Maybe because she knew someday her grandchildren would look at those snapshots and say, "Boy, what a bunch of geeks."

Nowadays I like to take a photograph of my three kids on the first day of school. (I admit that some years I don't quite get around to it till about March.) I take one because they're wearing new clothes, I survived the summer, and someday I want to have something really good to show my grandchildren. But also because starting something new is important.

Starting something new is a big part of life. I want Tom, Carrie, and Andy to get used to it. To accept it. To welcome it.

If I placed two of those photos—taken twenty-five years or more apart—side by side, the clothes would look different. The hairstyles wouldn't be the same. The shoes wouldn't match. But there's something identical, something in each child's eyes, something on each child's face.

Excitement.

Anxiety.

Fear.

Impatience.

Let's get going, already! Let me move on. Let me start grade school. The fourth grade. Junior high. High school.

Maybe some year I should take a photo after they come home on the first day of school. When the look says, "Holy cow! What have I gotten myself into this time? Why did I ever want to leave . . . ?"

Kindergarten. The primary grades. Grade school. Junior high. What was I thinking of? Sure, it was kind of boring, but this, this is . . .

Hard.

Just about the time my kids figure they're on top of the heap, they have to move on to a bigger heap. And start over again . . . at the bottom.

No one gets the wind knocked out of his or her sails faster—and more completely—than a freshman in high school. The poor ninth-grader has spent years, literally years, establishing a reputation, learning the ropes, getting it all under control. Years becoming one of the "big kids."

It's all wiped out in a day. At least it seems that way. It takes a while to establish a new foothold, to match the pace, to regain some confidence, and realize making that change was the right thing to do.

I want my children to know that even after they've graduated, there are going to be a lot of new beginnings. A lot of times when they have to move on. Graduation itself can be tough. You've made it! Way to go! And now . . . now what?

Finding and starting a new job is scary.

Getting married is scary.

Becoming a parent is . . . terrifying. That may be the first time when it becomes clear that having something also means giving up something. When you become a parent, you give up quite a bit you may have become accustomed to.

Freedom.

Money.

Sleep.

Privacy.

Sanity.

And then there are the bad days.

But, as every dad discovers, it is possible to get used to a lifestyle without those little trimmings.

Life never stands still. But through it all there is one constant: "'I am the Alpha and the Omega,' says the Lord God," St. John writes (Rv 1:8). At every beginning, at every ending, God is there.

At every birth.

At every death.

At every step between and beyond.

For a time I can be with my kids during their beginnings and endings. I can send them out with words of encouragement and love, and welcome them home the same way. In between, they're on their own. I can't walk into the classroom with them. I can't show up on the playground and tell the "big kids" to quit picking on them. I can't roam the neighborhood like their guardian angels.

But I can let them know that everyone starting something new is going to make mistakes, is going to have a tough time for a while. Everyone starting something new is going to experience a "rookie year" of one kind or another.

Then it will get easier.

It will get less challenging.

It will get comfortable.

It will get safe.

It will get to be time to move on, in one way or another.

I hope they realize that God will be there. That God is not just the Alpha and the Omega. He's the nudge between the old Omega and the new Alpha.

# Any Day
# Can Be Father's Day

"THERE'S MOTHER'S DAY and Father's Day," kids always point out to their parents. "Why isn't there Children's Day?"

When my three asked me about this, I, like every other parent, answered, "Every day is children's day."

Yeah, the smirks on their faces told me. Right.

I guess they could tell it was a standard line and there was no point arguing about it. It was just one of the ones they file away to use themselves when they have kids. (Along with "Because I said so," "I don't care what everyone else in the class is doing/wearing/going to do," and "Well, *I'm* cold. Now go put on a sweater.")

I suspect Father's Day lives on because greeting card companies really push it. Even though I've never seen a card offering what a dad really wants: a twenty-four-hour truce. Why doesn't Hallmark have a nice one with a big white flag on it? Inside it could say: "We love you, dear Dad, You're great as can be./For all of today,/We'll stop World War III."

It's not going to happen.

I have a theory about Father's Day. It's always celebrated in a better way than Mother's Day. (This is because of the Two Barber Rule. If you walk into a barber shop that has only two barbers and one guy's hair looks great and the other guy's hair looks like it was cut with a steak knife, choose the barber with the bad haircut. He's the one who did the nice job on the first fellow.)

Father's Day is better because a mother does the planning. A dad receives gifts that are wrapped in wrapping paper. A mom gets hers in that morning's comics.

"Dinner out" really is a good idea, but most husbands never think far enough ahead to make reservations at a nice restaurant. Instead, Dad ends up saying, "Why don't you get the large fries?" and "Let me carry that tray for you."

I like Father's Day because it gives me an opportunity— an excuse—to tell Tom, Carrie, and Andy that I like being their father. But over the years I've discovered that the tired, old Children's Day line can apply to dads.

Every day isn't Father's Day. But any day can become Father's Day.

When Tom and I head out on a cold winter's morning and I'm walking so carefully across the icy sidewalk and he laughs and runs and slides.

When I go into the boys' room and see a bent up VW hubcap leaning against Andy's dresser. A treasure he found when we were out on a walk together.

When I remember a "Happy Birthday" balloon—one of those silver jobs—Carrie got for me a few years ago. "It was her idea," Monica had told me. "She insisted." The helium is long gone, but the balloon is still on a bookshelf above my desk.

I don't remember any Father's Day with my father. I know there have been a lot of them, but they aren't what stand out in my mind. It's other times—everyday times— that I'll never forget.

There was the evening I was supposed to learn the twelve points of the Boy Scout law for some badge test. I can still recall them all: trustworthy, loyal, helpful, friendly, courteous, kind, obedient, cheerful, thrifty, brave, clean, and reverent.

Dad took the time to help me. He divided the traits into four groups of three and told me to think of somebody—or something—for each set. I know our dog was the first set and I was the last. He made it funny. He made it easy. He made it unforgettable.

I wouldn't be surprised if my children don't remember any official Father's Day. I hope together we're celebrating our own days. I hope we'll continue to do that for a long, long time.

God the Father has his day, too. The sabbath. The idea behind it—slow down, say thanks—is a good one, but it's gotten pretty watered down over the centuries. Too often now it's just a day off except for an hour in church.

An hour for religion.

I want my kids to come to realize that a relationship with God—and everyone has one whether he or she admits it or not—isn't something that can be limited to an hour a week. Limited to the "Lord's Day." That doesn't work any more than limiting a dad-child relationship to "Father's Day."

Father's Day, like the Lord's Day, celebrates something that already exists. It's a time to recall and give thanks for the many experiences that have already been shared and to pray for those yet to come. It's a formal time to say "I love you," but not a substitute for all the other times, for all the special days that belong to a father and his children.

# THIRTY-FOUR

# "Daddy,
# Why Do People Die?"

W HEN CARRIE WAS IN THE SIXTH GRADE, her fourth-grade teacher was diagnosed as having cancer and died a few months later. Monica and I could only hold our daughter and tell her we knew it hurt her more than the rest of us.

Hurt her more because she knew that teacher better than the rest of us. Because she loved that teacher.

Is eleven too young to learn that if you love someone, you run the risk of experiencing so much pain when you lose that someone?

I remember her teacher sitting in the back of church on Sunday mornings. She would smile and give a little wave as the five of us trooped by—Andy and Tom elbowing each other, trying to be first.

She was an ordinary person who lived a life of service. No fancy home or car. No big salary or title. But Jo-Ann Clayton was teaching Carrie a valuable lesson about what's really important. She was teaching me, too.

About a week after Jo-Ann died, the father of one of Andy's third-grade classmates passed away.

"Andy's worried about you," Monica told me when I got home from work that afternoon. "He's afraid you're going to die." Andy was in our bedroom trying to rest. I walked in and shut the door and sat down next to him. What could I say?

I'm fine, Andy. I'm not going to die.

Not right away.

At least, I think I'm not.

But someday I will. That's probably a long way off. Still, you never know. I didn't think that would go very far comforting him.

"Death is really ickey, huh?" I began.

He sniffed an "uh, huh."

"It doesn't make a lot of sense to me either," I said. "It doesn't seem fair that somebody you love has to leave. I know this has something to do with God's plan for us, but sometimes God's plan looks pretty stupid to us."

"God's plan looks really stupid to me!"

That was about all either of us needed to say. That was enough. Looking back, I don't know why I said what I said. I believe it, but I don't know why I said it. I think it must have been the Holy Spirit. For one brief moment, sitting there with my son, I had a bit of wisdom. It had to come from somewhere.

Andy had it, too. We could agree we don't like death, and it hurts people who are left behind. But God is in the middle of it somehow. God's plan for us is more than just the time we spend on earth.

And we saw it as God's plan. We knew death wasn't a bad thing for the person who died.

Then Andy's tears began again. I don't remember if I held him. I hope I did.

"I'm crying for Peter," he said, naming his classmate.

I didn't have any more words for him. I just loved him. I marveled at the compassion a young child can demonstrate.

The five of us went to the funeral. Later, at a luncheon that followed in the gymnasium, I told Andy to go say hello to Peter.

"Just let him know you're here," I said. He gave me a look

that said "I don't want to!"

"Just do it," I said. "He needs to know you're here."

The two boys only said hi to each other before the meal, but afterwards they played basketball with a group of children. The other kids were bigger than they were which forced them to work together. Whenever either one snagged a rebound, both would squeal with delight. Finally, they gave up and sat down on the stage and watched the big kids play. Sat side-by-side.

When we were driving home, I thanked Andy for what he had done. He said they enjoyed the basketball game, and when they were watching the other kids Peter had talked a bit about his dad. Nothing monumental. Just a little incident.

Almost a year later, when I was interviewing the director of a Catholic cemeteries program for a newspaper article, I heard the term "grief ministry" and I thought of those two eight-year-olds on that stage. It seemed like a pretty lofty title for one kid saying hi to the other and playing a little basketball. But the description fit. It was one person making an effort to reach out to another who had lost a loved one. It was overcoming the fear that surrounds death, the worry about saying the wrong thing, the awkwardness, the embarrassment, the hesitation.

It was a classic example of a basic definition Christians have had for almost two thousand years: "See how they love one another."

There's another fact about death that I hope my children—and I—always recognize. Love is something that death can never conquer. I can continue to love someone who has died. That person can continue to love me through their prayers and support in heaven. That's something that Catholics believe. It's something I believe.

Monica's paternal grandparents are buried on the edge of a little town about one hundred miles east of Seattle. Their cemetery plots are near a grove of pine trees. They loved the outdoors, the Northwest.

When we visit their graves, the kids run into the woods

and bring back pine cones. They surround the headstone with them. They know their mom is going to cry a little bit and laugh a little bit. They know she loved her grandparents and they loved her.

It's obvious their love hasn't ended, and now it includes the kids and me, too. Someday you'll get to meet Grandma and Grandpa, Monica tells Tom, Carrie, and Andy. Someday we'll all be together forever.

"On that day," I need to add the next time we're visiting the cemetery, "on that day, God's plan—the one we thought was so stupid—will make perfect sense."

# THIRTY-FIVE

# The Sex Talk

"**D**ADDY, WHERE DID I COME FROM?"
"Uh, . . ."

Every father faces—and stumbles over—that one when his kids are still pretty little. I really doubt that my three remember what my answers were. I don't.

Tom would have been the easiest because he's adopted. "Where did you come from? The agency."

But with Carrie and Andy, I hope I didn't say something like "God made you and Mommy and I helped."

That's the truth, of course, but the "I helped" part might have really worried them. Even as preschoolers they were familiar with my lack of skills at any kind of building or fixing.

"Daddy helped make me? Oh, no! What part is going to fall off first?"

As they got older, I realized that talking about sex with the kids was a lot easier when they were little and didn't care about sex. But they need to know and Monica and I, as parents, have an obligation to explain things to them. Explain things from a Catholic perspective because that's what we believe. Our explanations can be very different than the ones they would pick up from other sources.

The nitty-gritty discussions—the mechanics—have been divided according to gender. Female with female and male with male. No one has objected to this. Maybe that was Monica's doing. That way she needed to talk to only one child and I had two. No matter. I agreed with her.

And now that we've cleared that hurdle, I'm discovering—once again—that was easy compared to what comes next. Or, rather, what came with it and continues to come. Which is:

Physically, this is what sex is all about. But sex is more than the physical. And the value system that we follow, that we believe in, says the physical should not happen without these other conditions.

Well, now, that certainly sounds vague. At best.

We say you don't have sexual intercourse with someone unless you're married to that someone. We say, once you're married to that someone, you don't have sexual intercourse with anyone else.

Huh?

Only go to bed with your spouse.

It doesn't matter what's presented on a "Night Court" rerun or "Top Gun" VCR tape or Top 40 tune. It doesn't matter what's implied—often not too subtly—in a television commercial for pickup trucks or a magazine ad for shave cream.

Sometimes sending out that Christian message seems almost useless because the world's message—used so frequently because sex sells—is everywhere. It's comforting to think that our children's attitudes may have less to do with what Monica and I have said and more to do with how we live.

I hope my kids know that doesn't mean she and I are above other people. Far from it. I hope I know that, too. It means that what other people do doesn't determine what we do. (That standard parent line comes to mind: "If everyone in your class was jumping off a bridge does that mean . . .?") Equally, if not more important, is the fact that while we are supposed to judge what's right and wrong, we are in no position to judge others. It's wrong to judge them. That's up to God.

Why marriage? A couple of reasons. The first is it takes guts to stand up in front of other people and say, "I love this person and I want to live with this person for the rest of my life."

The second is grace, the special blessings and help that come with a sacrament. Marriage is a sacrament. The church doesn't talk about the sacrament of "wedding," it talks about the sacrament of marriage. The ceremony takes about an hour. Living out those promises takes a lifetime. For better or for worse.

Even under the best of circumstances, sometimes that isn't easy. Sometimes life isn't easy. That's when there is no substitute for grace. As a husband and a father, I want all I can get.

I need all I can get.

I think having sex at a young age outside marriage is like racing a car down the freeway just because you're tall enough to reach the pedals. The odds of getting hurt and hurting someone else are tremendous. You've got to follow the manufacturer's instructions, or you're asking for trouble. That means respecting the way God set up sexuality to work, even if that means waiting and showing some good, old fashioned self-control. Some of the dangers are physical—AIDS and other diseases, pregnancy—but there are also emotional, psychological, and spiritual dangers.

At the same time, there are so many pressures on teens to "take a test ride." Some people would have my kids believe sex can never hurt. Those people are lying. Some people would say abuses of sex—like prostitution and pornography—are harmless. That they are victimless crimes. That's simply not true.

So often, so very often, the young men and women in those photographs, the young men and women out on the street, were the victims of sexual abuse when they were children. It's not unusual for that abuse to have happened in their own homes. That a father, stepfather, other relative, or mom's boyfriend was the abuser.

Now as adults, their view of sex has been mangled.

Their sense of self-worth all but destroyed.

That doesn't mean they are beyond hope. It doesn't mean they do not have opportunities and obligations to change their behavior. It does mean it's so much harder for them than it would be for someone who hasn't been hurt that way.

There's also tremendous pressure on parents to back off from standards of right and wrong in dealing with their teenagers in this volatile area. After all, they're young men and women who need to make their own choices in life. Who am I to tell them what to do?—or so the argument goes.

But a loving parent who understands the consequences of such important decisions *won't* give in to the pressure to back off. No, a loving parent will help a young adult make sound, informed choices. At times, that'll mean taking a stand and being unpopular. At other times, it'll mean sitting down with your kids and sharing about the beauty of sexuality in marriage—even if you're embarrassed and would rather not.

I don't want my children to be mesmerized by the glitz of sex that's used to sell products. I also don't want them to think that, by definition, sex is evil and sinful.

I hope instead that someday, in marriage, they know the special touch, the special word, the special love—the special grace and gift from God—that sex is and was meant to be.

THIRTY-SIX

# Catholicism Is Not a Spectator Sport

ANDY WAS STILL A LITTLE GUY, a fan of Mr. Rogers, when he first began to sit down and watch ball games on TV. Not necessarily interesting games. Any games. The Seattle Mariners, for instance. Even in late August when they were in the cellar and were going to stay there for the rest of the season.

It took me a while to figure out why. Not why the Mariners had a poor record. Why Andy would stay on that sofa and pay such close attention.

Sometimes I'd take all three kids over to the high school and make them go around the track a few times. Then we'd hang around for part of a baseball game.

Andy loved it. It didn't matter to him that the players were only in high school. They looked old enough to him to be in the pros. Just like to me, a lot of pros look young enough to be in high school.

But at any age, right on down to Little Leaguers, some players are extremely talented. Players who are a joy to watch. They make it look so easy.

Effortless.

They make it look fun.

Those players—pros or peewees—were the ones Andy

145

has taught me to look for. He knows that one great hit, one terrific catch, one blinding pitch, can make a whole game worthwhile. It seems funny to say, but sports have helped teach my kids that life isn't always in high gear.

Sometimes things go slow. Sometimes a player waits and waits and waits. And then—BOOM!—when the ball comes his way, he's ready. Eager.

Part of the reason I like watching games with Tom, Carrie, and Andy is that so many analogies apply. Life can mean ...

A grand slam.

A "Hail Mary" touchdown.

A three-point shot at the buzzer.

But then, too, there's strike three.

Fumbling.

Fouling out.

The sports they like to watch most are the ones that they play. Golf is not a favorite. Bowling never made it until Tom joined the Special Olympics bowling team.

I think the same is true for their religion. If all they do is watch, they aren't going to be very interested. They aren't going to pay attention for very long. Fortunately, Catholicism is not a spectator sport. They have to get in the game— feed the hungry, shelter the homeless, and so on—if religion is going to make sense.

If not, to them Mass will seem a lot like a thirty-six-hole golf tournament on the tube. Week after week after week.

I hope they notice that, just like in sports, there are some stars in the Catholic church. There have been—and there still are—people who make it look so easy. Make it look like so much fun.

"This is what Christ said," they tell others when asked about how they live. "So this is why I do the things I do."

And just like in sports, it's always the basics. The best players—the best Christians—just follow the basics.

Love God.

Love your neighbor as you love yourself.

No mystery.

You want to make a foul shot, you do this, this, and this.

You want to get a base hit, you do this, this, and this.

You want to catch a pass, you do this, this, and this.

You want to be a Catholic . . .

You want to be a Catholic, you don't sit over on the sidelines. You get in the game. And your performance is going to improve the longer you play, the longer you practice. A "practicing Catholic" can mean you don't have it right yet, but you're working on it.

# THIRTY-SEVEN

# "Oh, Yeah? Well, I Hate Homework, Too!"

I GRADUATED FROM COLLEGE IN 1974 and thought I would never have homework again. That just goes to prove how really stupid a college graduate can be. I was wrong. Very wrong. I have homework at least four nights out of seven. Sometimes I get Friday, Saturday, and Sunday off.

I hate Monday through Thursday.

I hate homework.

Still.

I have homework because I have children who have homework. Worse yet, I want them to have it. I know they need it. I know it's good for them. I laugh when they tell me their teachers have really piled it on today.

"Good!" I say to Tom, Carrie, and Andy. "A good teacher is one who really piles on the old homework."

And I think to myself, "Why did she have to pile on the old homework today! I hate homework!"

Sometimes that's the trouble with being a dad. You can see both sides of the coin at the same time. A trick that makes me and all the other fathers in the world mentally cross-eyed.

"Can you check my math?" Andy will ask. That's a tough one because I can't answer, "Look it up." So I check Andy's math and since he can't use a calculator, neither can I. I need to show him how important it is to be able to divide 37659.01 by 136 without a battery-operated device.

Tom, on the other hand, never has homework.

"Do you have any homework tonight?" I ask.

"Huh, uh."

"Then I want you to write a hundred and fifty word paper for me," I say. "Tell me something about your day. Whatever you like."

This is the battering ram Monica and I and Tom's teachers have devised to get through the "no homework tonight" blockade.

"A hundred and fifty!" Tom says. "How come a hundred and fifty?"

"I thought two hundred was too many," I answer.

"I got homework," he then says and starts to begin to get ready to prepare himself for doing his homework. Soon.

Carrie tries to be logical about it. "Why?" she asks, whatever the assignment is. For example, "Why do I have to learn Washington state history?"

"Because we live in Washington state."

"Did you have to learn Washington state history?"

"Not when I lived in Iowa."

"Like this part," she says, pointing at a worksheet. "Name four famous mountain men."

"That was one of the hardest ones in Iowa state history," I say.

I remember doing a paper on the Middle Ages in the sixth grade. I've never mentioned this to my kids because I know they will make some crack like, "A current affairs report?" It was due on a Monday and Mom was helping me late on a Sunday afternoon. I suppose the teacher had given the class more than one weekend to write it. That little detail has slipped my memory.

Mom and I were sitting at the dining room table and I was

mumbling and grumbling and I said, "I don't want to do this." She answered, "Sometimes you have to do things you don't want to do."

For years I thought she had been talking to me. Now, I'm almost convinced she was talking to herself. She didn't want to spend her Sunday afternoon with some eleven-year-old who didn't want to write a paper on the Middle Ages. I remember very little about the Middle Ages, but I did learn two things from that assignment. First, sometimes you have to do things you don't want to do. And second, you *can* do things you don't want to do.

I can accomplish a task—I can do a good job—even when I don't want to do the job at all. I want my children to learn the facts and pick up the skills from doing homework, which is always a battle.

I also want them to learn about doing things they don't want to do. I want them to learn that if they only do what they feel like doing, only what they like to do, they aren't going to get a lot done. A lot that needs to be done. Life makes demands, and we all have to answer those demands.

What if I don't feel like staying up late tonight with a child who has the flu?

What if I don't feel like paying all my bills this month?

What if I don't feel like doing what the boss tells me to do?

Life will challenge them on many different fronts and I want them to be prepared. I want them to have confidence. I want them to have the ability to motivate themselves. I want them to learn that often a big task is accomplished by completing a series of very little tasks.

Leading a good life, for example.

God gives me homework to help me with that one. He gives me things to do that will help me know him better and love others around me more. Sometimes I don't like a particular assignment. It's too hard. I don't want to do it now and why do I have to do it anyway? What good is this going to do me? Why do I have to learn this?

God gives me things to do that can make me a better father.

A better Christian.

A better person.

I may grumble and complain, "Oh, yeah? Well, I think that is one really stupid idea and I don't want to do it. I'm not going to do it. You can't make me do it." Sometimes I sound just like my kids when they talk about their homework.

What's important is if I end up doing it. That's what really matters.

Jesus told a parable that made that point (Mt 21:28-31). A man had two sons. He told the first one, "Go on out and work in the field"; and the son answered, "In your dreams, Pop." But then he went and did the work. Then the father went to the second one and said, "Go on out and work in the field." The son answered, "Sure, no sweat, on my way right now." But he never went. "Which did the father's will?" Jesus asked his followers. The answer was pretty obvious.

I suspect that all their lives my kids will hate their homework.

That's all right. So will I.

I pray that all their lives, my kids will do their homework. Will do God's work.

# "Are We Having Fun Yet?"

S TRING CHEESE. Sourdough bread. Strawberries.
That's how my kids describe fun in San Francisco. That is the "perfect" meal.

We drove there from Seattle a number of summers ago. It was a spur-of-the-moment idea. I was still working at a newspaper and had two weeks vacation, so we just packed up and went.

I suppose Monica and I could have planned it. But then Andy wasn't quite three, Carrie was six, and Tom hadn't turned eight yet, so we had only one plan and it was pretty basic: survive.

Basic, not simple.

One of my best memories of that trip was when we drove into the Fisherman's Wharf district our first night there and found an empty parking space right in front of us.

Miracles do happen.

The kids don't remember that. Their memories of the traditional tourist sights are a little vague, too.

We spent each night at a campground about sixty miles north of the city. It was the closest, cheapest place for a family that doesn't plan far enough ahead to make reservations. One morning we left the campground late and stopped at a little store to buy something for lunch.

String cheese. Sourdough bread. Strawberries.

I know it wasn't that meal that made the trip so memorable. It was the trip that made the meal so important. It was being together and really enjoying each other's company. The right people can transform a meal, a house, a life.

I need to remember that when the five of us are in the middle of some grand adventure that is supposed to be fun but is a long way from it. Every dad has been there. When the troops turn to him and they ask, one way or another, "Are we having fun yet?"

Dad knows the answer: "I don't know about you guys, but I'm not."

I think most dads also know that the family has to make time to do things together, has to try to have some kind of fun, if it's going to happen at all. And it has to be everybody. That's not easy to arrange when family members are scattered so much of the time.

Work.

School.

Church stuff.

Sports.

Babysitting.

Overnight at friends' houses.

Each family has a unique combination of obligations and interests. For most it's a long list, which grows as the kids get older. I know it's not unusual for some families to say they seldom, if ever, even share a meal together.

It takes work to have fun as a family.

It takes planning.

Most of the time it means everyone has to give up something to be a part of it. (Not just money, Dad. Although that comes to mind first.) Every member has to make some kind of investment in this "Stupid Plan That Nobody Likes and Just Whose Idea Was It in the First Place?"

Blame Mom.

That's what I always do.

"Come on, you guys. This means a lot to your mother."

Fun has never come knocking at our front door. (With maybe the exception of the pizza delivery person. But even then we had to call first.) We have to find it. We have to create it. We have to set ourselves up to let it happen. And then it slides in where a father least expects it.

The kids and I went walking around Green Lake one Saturday morning. It's in a popular Seattle park and there are always a lot of walkers, joggers, bikers, and roller-skaters along the two-and-a-half mile road that circles the lake.

But on that day as far as fun goes . . . nothing.

We went over to an indoor pool and watched some people swim laps. Nothing.

We went into the gym and watched part of a basketball game. Nothing.

By then they wanted food. What's with kids today? You feed them and then a couple of hours later they want to eat again.

They had a lot of great suggestions: hamburgers, pizza, fish and chips. I had very little money, so we walked over to a local grocery store.

All right, here it comes. String cheese, sourdough bread, and strawberries, right? String cheese, yes. It was on sale. Sourdough bread cost too much so we got flour tortillas. Strawberries? In Seattle in the middle of winter? No way! Eat an apple. And, as a little bonus because no one had complained too loudly, a bag of fat chocolate cookies.

Then it was back to the park, sit down at a picnic table and . . . nothing.

A bird landed nearby. I don't remember if it was a sparrow, a crow, a pigeon, or a seagull. One of the kids threw a bit of tortilla at it. Suddenly the food was flying and then all kinds of birds were swooping in. (They did not eat pieces of apple; they were not given pieces of cookie.)

A preschooler and his mom walked by and watched for a while. Then one of my kids handed the mother a half of a tortilla and the little guy squealed as he fed the flock at his feet. We watched and laughed and talked about when Tom, Carrie, and Andy were little.

I think the Holy Family had that kind of fun, too. That they enjoyed each other's company and did things that would seem a little silly or foolish to everyone else. Corny. "You had to be there" is true a lot of times when it comes to family fun.

None of that's recorded in the Gospels. But in Luke 2:51-52, right after Mary and Joseph find the boy Jesus teaching in the temple, the evangelist writes: "He went down with them and came to Nazareth and was obedient to them; and his mother kept all these things in her heart. And Jesus advanced [in] wisdom and age and favor before God and men."

Of course, Mary remembered the big things, the ones that are written in the Gospel. But I bet that's not all. I bet there were the little things, too. The unexpected ones. The simple, fun ones. The ones that are just as much a gift from God. The ones that make being a parent like nothing else on earth.

# THIRTY-NINE

# Sacraments: Special Times for God's Special Gifts

I DON'T REMEMBER MUCH ABOUT the baptisms of my three children. I'm sure my brother baptized each of them, but a dad's world is a bit of a blur right after a baby is born.

Mine is still a little fuzzy.

Recently I saw a photo that was taken at Andy's baptism. Monica is holding the baby, and I have a death grip on the other two kids. Carrie was three and Tom wasn't quite five.

"No wonder we were always tired," I said to Monica as I looked at what was, truly, a handful of kids. "No wonder I don't remember much from the early 1980s."

I do remember having a new child was a reason to celebrate. Here was a brand new person. Never been seen before. Never been before. And he or she was going to be living with us. I was this kid's daddy.

Amazing.

One of my favorite parts about being a Catholic is that the church takes moments like that—very human moments— and provides a way to celebrate them. God provides extra grace just when a dad needs it most.

In my early years of grade school, I learned that "a sacrament is an outward sign instituted by Christ to give grace." I knew what most of those words meant. Except maybe "instituted." But it wasn't until I was a lot older that the words started to really make sense. It wasn't until much later that I began to appreciate the beauty and simplicity of the sacraments.

Simple words and simple symbols. Words, water, bread, wine, oil, salt. No magic or exotic ingredients. Everyday items that can help me—and, I hope, my kids—realize that God is a part of my everyday life. Help us realize that during the big moments of our lives, God is there.

When a child is born.

Growing older and accepting responsibility, owning up to mistakes that hurt people.

Living day-to-day, trying to do the right thing.

Becoming an adolescent, standing on the threshold of adulthood.

Getting married or choosing a life of service as a priest.

Facing illness and acknowledging death is part of life.

Baptism. Reconciliation. Eucharist. Confirmation. Marriage. Priesthood. Anointing of the Sick.

"Instituted" by Christ. Begun by Christ. Seven gifts to his followers to help them with their lives. Gifts that have been handed down from one generation to the next for almost two thousand years. Gifts that provide ways for the Holy Spirit to touch an individual's life. Gifts that "give grace."

Grace?

Now how do I explain grace to my kids? How do I understand it myself? I can't say what it is exactly, but I can say what it's like.

"Remember the TV show 'Knight Rider'?" I can ask my kids.

Uh, huh.

"How the fancy car would be going along and then the guy would launch into 'turbo' power?"

Uh, huh.

"Grace is like turbo power."

Now I'm pretty sure Thomas Aquinas didn't put it that way but . . .

"Keeping in touch with God is like making sure you have fuel in your fancy car. It's what makes it go. Sometimes you need a little extra oomph and so you push the turbo power button. God knows you need more zip at some points in your life and so he's provided the juice to give you an extra boost."

As my children get older, they're going to need more zip. I want them to know its source. I want them to know there is a never-ending supply that is theirs for the asking.

I want them to know that the sacraments will help them grow spiritually. That, just as they can mature physically, intellectually, and emotionally, they can grow spiritually. They can become spiritually stronger.

The sacraments are there to help us better understand what God wants us to do and more easily do it. More readily do it. He has given us the sacraments to help us meet the challenges that life brings. To overcome those challenges. To grow from those challenges.

I love walking up to Communion behind my three kids. I love watching them hold out their hands and accept the consecrated host. I love hearing them answer "Amen" when the priest or the Eucharistic minister says, "The Body of Christ."

Christ and the church give my children so much more than I can give them, and I want only the best for my kids. I know that's what they're receiving in the sacraments. I know that, filled with God's turbo power, nothing can stop them.

# FORTY

# What I Want
# My Kids to Remember

I 'VE HEARD GUYS DESCRIBED AS "successful" and knew exactly what that meant. These fellows made money. No matter what field they were in—insurance, banking, real estate, plumbing, auto repair—they kept getting promoted and making a higher salary, or the business they began took off and was always in the black.

Their success had nothing to do with their families. At best, they might also be known as "good providers."

Again, the measurement is based on money. A good provider gives his family a nice home, newer cars, snappy clothes, deluxe vacations, and on and on. My problem is that sometimes I believe that. I start walking down that path. If I can make this amount of money writing one book, how much can I make doing three?

How many articles can I crank out in a month?

How many newspapers can I write columns for?

And then, with just a little more money, I could give my family . . . What?

After the basics are covered—food, clothing, shelter, education, transportation, health insurance—how much do I really need? How much do my three kids need? And how much is my chasing those dollars going to cost them?

I want to be financially successful. I believe most dads want the same thing. ("Wouldn't it be nice if ... ?") But I also know that unless I stop and think about it, pray about it, I easily confuse success with excess.

It's more important to my children that I be a successful father than a successful writer. I am absolutely convinced they will never stand over my grave and say, "Boy, I sure remember the advance he got for that one book. Yes, siree, that was really something. And the royalty percentage! The number of copies sold! What a dad!"

Jesus put it very simply: "You can't serve two masters" (Mt 6:24).

Either I'm concerned about getting stinking rich or I'm concerned about other people, including my kids. I can't have it both ways. It's not possible.

Or to rewrite another famous quote: "What does it profit a man to become CEO but lose his family?"

Lose his very soul.

In 1986 I met Pope John Paul II. Right there at the Vatican. In a private audience (with a hundred other people). That was when I was editor of a diocesan newspaper and the pope had just ordained the diocese's new auxiliary bishop. When it was my turn to say hello, I stuck out my hand and smiled. I hope. I'm not really sure what I did. I know we shook hands. I have photos of that. But I think I was tongue-tied.

My children will not mention that over my grave.

They will not fight over who gets the photo of Dad and John Paul II.

What will my children say? I'd put my money—the little I have and the much I owe—on something like: "I remember when Dad took me up on the roof."

We live in a one-story house and about once a year, the pine needles and moss have to be swept off the roof. So I climb a homemade ladder and work a while. Soon there are kids at the bottom of the ladder asking to come up.

So I let them.

One at a time.

Each walks around up there a while and giggles and checks out the view and calls down to the others still yammering to get their turn.

I believe that—and other earth-shaking experiences very similar to that—is what my children will remember of me.

I believe those experiences will in some way determine if I am a successful father. At the top of the list will be: he loved us.

That, in the end, is the only item that truly matters.

I believe I am a successful father if my children know I love them. And as we all get older, I'm beginning to realize that big things turn out to mean very little. And the little things turn out to be very big.

A newer car means less than everyone helping hang the Christmas lights along the front gutter.

The perfect, "I-gotta-have-'em" running shoes are soon worn out, tossed, and forgotten, but the memories of all of us, together, making a haul trick-or-treating can still make us smile. (Daddy liked Snickers. No one liked little boxes of raisins.)

Together, my children and I can create those times. Together we can build a treasure that can never be lost, stolen, or destroyed. A treasure that money can't buy.

# FORTY-ONE

# Easter:
# The End of the Story

H OLY WEEK WAS MADE FOR KIDS. It's filled with visual aids
and everybody gets a speaking part. Each of the "big
days"—Passion Sunday (Palm Sunday), Holy Thursday,
Good Friday, and Easter Sunday—is different. But sometimes my children say "Do we gotta go to church again?"

Sometimes I have the same question myself.

There's a lot of going to church. That's for sure. But there's
a lot that happened that first Holy Week that needs to be
remembered.

I've never asked them, but I'd bet Tom, Carrie, and Andy
like Christmas better than Easter. At Christmas you get two
weeks vacation and presents.

Beat that!

Easter hasn't been as commercialized as Christmas has.
There are the Easter bunny and chocolate eggs (and those
horrible marshmallow chicks). Maybe a few people send
Easter cards and get a new oufit but it can't compare to the
Christmas shopping blitz.

So how come the church says Easter is the most important
feast of the year? Without Easter, Christ's coming down to
earth is more like just a cute story. Sort of a religious "E.T."
Easter—Christ's rising from the dead—is what makes the

Gospels the "good news." Good Friday is what makes Easter possible.

Passion Sunday always surprises my kids. We walk into church and the vestibule has tables stacked with green palm branches.

You have to get a good one. I've learned that over the years. You can't make a hasty decision. It's better to really dig through that mound and find just the right one. (The "right one" is always bigger and longer than the ones chosen by your siblings.)

Then during Mass, you get to wave the branch around. Like you were at a Seattle Seahawks game. We've never done "the wave" at our parish, but it wouldn't be too out of place. That's the point of the branches, I tell my kids. Think of them as cheap pompons or banners. On the first Passion Sunday, people twirled them around and tossed them and their coats in front of Christ—like a red carpet—and shouted "WAY TO GO, JESUS! ALL RIGHT! YOU'RE NUMBER ONE! YOU'RE NUMBER ONE! YOU'RE NUMBER ONE!"

And you get to take the palm branches home with you. Some people know how to weave them into beautiful works of art. I have shown my children how to roll a branch up, put a rubber band around it, let it sit for a week or so, take the rubber band off, unroll it and notice the lovely curl it has. Looking very much like a palm branch that was rolled up and held together by a rubber band for a week or so.

They were definitely not impressed.

I don't remember taking Tom, Carrie, and Andy to a Holy Thursday service. I know they would like part of it: the part where the pastor (just like the bishop and the pope, yes, the pope!) washes some people's feet.

No!

Right in church.

Why?

That's what Christ did.

No!

He washed his disciples' feet. He acted like a servant to show them how they should act. How my children should act. How I should act.

On Holy Thursday we remember the first Mass. We remember Jesus giving himself under the form of bread and wine. At each Mass we remember Holy Thursday, Good Friday, and Easter Sunday: Christ dying and rising. The same Christ—was born in a stable, preached in the temple when he was still a kid, fed the people with loaves and fishes, called the apostles, was beaten up and executed, and came back to life—this is who my children receive at Mass.

The very same one.

Holy Week helps me remember that. Holy Week helps me teach my children that.

On Holy Thursday things are going great. Yes, Judas skips out and Jesus tells Peter that Peter is going to deny him ("No way, Jesus! Get real!"), but other than that it was one terrific evening. Then it's off to the garden for a little praying. Jesus is terribly frightened about what's going to happen; the apostles he brought with him just conk out and go to sleep.

I think the kids and I now have an idea of how they felt. One year Monica signed us up to visit the church from five to six on Good Friday morning. The Blessed Sacrament was left out and parishioners were asked to make a half-hour commitment.

"No sense getting up so early for just half an hour, right?" Monica said to us.

"Uhhhh, . . ." the four of us answered.

It was cold going out that early in the morning. And dark. It was hard to stay awake for an hour. It was easy to imagine how the apostles felt. Except they were frightened, too. After Jesus was arrested they didn't know what would happen to him. What would happen to them.

"Jesus who?" Peter answered when some folks asked, "Don't you know that guy?"

I find it comforting that the number one apostle, the first

pope, blew it. It gives me hope for the times I blow it. When, by my words or my actions—or my lack of words, my lack of action—I say, "Jesus who?" I want my children to know that story. I want it to give them hope, too.

Look what Peter did.

And look what he went on to do.

He messed up, but he didn't let it stop him. He ended up giving his life rather than give up his faith in Christ as the Messiah.

At church on Good Friday my kids and I shout, "CRUCIFY HIM!" Over and over again. I hate that. Just a few days earlier we were waving palm branches and cheering "YOU'RE NUMBER ONE!"

"CRUCIFY HIM!"

Would I die for my wife and my three children? I hope so.

Would I die for strangers? I doubt it.

For a single stranger? Probably not.

"CRUCIFY HIM!"

Jesus died for all of us. Jesus died for each of us. Jesus died for my wife and my children. Jesus died for me.

"CRUCIFY HIM!" I shout. "CRUCIFY HIM!"

I need to tell my kids: Jesus loves you, Tom, Carrie, and Andy. He loves you more than I ever will, and I don't know how that's possible. I just know it's true.

But that sadness, that shame and despair, of Good Friday aren't the end of the story. There's Easter Sunday. Christ rising from the dead. Coming back to life. The first one to come back. And everyone in Christ is going to rise again, to be together forever.

We share our little house now, but it won't always be that way. We'll be apart for a while—and it may seem like a long while when we're in the middle of that—but it won't be forever.

Remember that someday you and Mom and I will be together forever by the grace of God.

With God forever.

That's what Easter means.

And that will be the end of our story. That will be when we finally realize—finally truly believe—our time together with each other and with our God is never going to end.

God, the perfect Father, has planned the perfect ending.

Special Introductory Offer

# NEW COVENANT

*The Magazine of Catholic Renewal*

Month by month, *New Covenant* will bring you inspiration, teaching, and personal testimony that will help you:

- deepen your prayer life
- better understand your Catholic faith
- live as a Christian in today's world

Just write to the address below for a free copy of *New Covenant*. If you like what you see, pay the invoice and you'll receive eleven more copies–one year of *New Covenant* for only $14.95.

**NEW COVENANT**
Department S
P.O. Box 7009
Ann Arbor, MI 48107

## Another Book of Interest to Catholic Families

### Keeping Your Kids Catholic
*Edited by Bert Ghezzi*

The scenario could be replayed in many Catholic homes with a different cast of characters and props. Your sixteen-year-old son would rather watch rock videos than go to Mass. Your eleven-year-old daughter complains about going to confession.

You wax nostalgic for the "good old days" when it seemed easier to grow up Catholic. Though keeping your kids Catholic may seem impossible in the 1990s, Bert Ghezzi believes it can be done. In *Keeping Your Kids Catholic*, Catholic parents, religious educators, family counselors, and youth workers offer practical articles that cover nearly every aspect of Catholic family life. From a how-to article on sharing your faith with small children to articles on how to love adult children who leave the church, here is tested pastoral wisdom for raising your kids Catholic.  *$7.95*

Available at your Christian bookstore or from:
Servant Publications • Dept. 209 • P.O. Box 7455
Ann Arbor, Michigan 48107
Please include payment plus $1.25 per book
for postage and handling.
*Send for our FREE catalog of Christian
books, music, and cassettes.*